GRAMMAR SUCCESS
in 20 Minutes a Day

Other Titles of Interest from LearningExpress

Algebra Success in 20 Minutes a Day
Biology Success in 20 Minutes a Day
Chemistry Success in 20 Minutes a Day
Earth Science Success in 20 Minutes a Day
Physics Success in 20 Minutes a Day
Practical Math Success in 20 Minutes a Day
Reading Comprehension Success
Reasoning Skills Success in 20 Minutes a Day
Statistics Success in 20 Minutes a Day
Trigonometry Success in 20 Minutes a Day
Vocabulary and Spelling Success

GRAMMAR SUCCESS
in 20 Minutes a Day

Third Edition

LEARNINGEXPRESS®

NEW YORK

Library of Congress Cataloging-in-Publication Data

Grammar success in 20 minutes a day.—Third edition.
    pages cm
  ISBN 978-1-57685-931-5
  1. English language—Grammar—Problems, exercises, etc.   I. LearningExpress (Organization).
II. Title: Grammar success in twenty minutes a day.
  PE1112.G676 2013
  428.2—dc23

                                   2013026866

Printed in the United States of America

9 8 7 6 5 4 3 2 1

ISBN: 978-1-57685-931-5

For information on LearningExpress, other LearningExpress products, or bulk sales, please write to us at
  LearningExpress
  80 Broad Street
  Suite 400
  New York, NY 10004

Or visit us at
  www.learningexpressllc.com

9/43
BUT

CONTENTS ▶

CONTENTS

CONTENTS

INTRODUCTION ▶

Do your grammar skills need some brushing up? Perhaps you have an exam on the horizon, or maybe you want to hone your grammar skills to improve your writing or speech. Whatever the case may be, this quick reference guide will help put you well on your way toward accomplishing your grammar goals—no matter how big or small.

Because English is so complex, rules and guidelines called grammar and usage are necessary to help us better understand its many idiosyncrasies. While language is forever changing to meet our needs, the inner workings of a sentence are, for the most part, as constant as the stars, and figuring out these dynamics is like putting a puzzle together (or taking it apart).

Understanding the inner workings of a sentence can help you with your speech and writing—the essence of communication and language. And the benefits you get for your efforts far outweigh the 20 minutes of your day you'll spend with this book.

Before you begin to progress through the book, take the pretest on the next few pages to determine what you already know and what you might need to focus on. You might be surprised by just how much you remember!

PRETEST ▶

Before you start your study of grammar skills, get an idea of how much you already know and how much you need to learn by taking the pretest that follows. It consists of 50 multiple-choice questions about what is in this book. Naturally, 50 questions can not cover every single concept or rule you will learn by working through these lessons, so even if you answer all the questions correctly, it is almost guaranteed that you will find a few things in the book you did not already know. If you get lots of answers wrong on the pretest, do not worry—this book will teach you how to improve your grammar and writing, step by step.

Record your answers in this book. If it does not belong to you, list the numbers 1–50 on a piece of paper and write your answers there. Take as much time as you need to finish the test. When you finish, check your answers against the answer key that follows the test. Each answer lists the lesson of the book that covers the concept(s) in that question. If you get a high score on the pretest, you may be able to spend less time with this book than you originally planned. If you get a low score, you may find you will need more than 20 minutes a day to learn all that you need to know. Good luck!

Pretest

1. Circle the common nouns.

chair	joy	knitted
Australia	supermarket	Ohio
Monticello	understanding	toddlers
saucepan	dancing	hostess

2. Circle the abstract nouns.

peace	telephone	livelihood
deceit	cheerfulness	jungle
NASA	smile	rubber band
test	eyelash	patience

3. Circle the proper nouns.

Texas	Work	Clock
Puzzle	Nancy	Mr. Klondike
Licorice	Mexico City	Basketball
IBM	Spiderman	Mt. Everest

4. Circle the nouns that are pluralized correctly.

halves	theorys	oxen
casinoes	inchs	dishes
valleyes	houses	mother-in-laws
booths	tooths	hippopotamuses

5. Circle the hyphenated nouns that are spelled correctly.

sister-in-laws	kilowatt-hours
runner-ups	forget-me-nots
follow-ups	sticks-in-the-mud

6. Circle the nouns that have been made possessive correctly.

child's	her's	Jody's
Congress'	tooth's	cactus's
puppies'	moms'	Jason's
women's	his'	dress's

7. Circle the antecedents/pronouns that agree in gender.

tree/it	Anthony/she
King Henry/he	passenger/it
kangaroo/his	Alice/her

8. Circle the antecedents/pronouns that agree in number.

kids/him	everybody/they
Kathy and I/it	fish/they
group/it	fish/it
each/he or she	women/we
both/they	

9. Circle the interrogative pronouns.

who	when	whose
which	whom	whomever
how	where	what

10. Circle the subjective case pronouns.

I went to his house and saw him.
She brought me an apple and I thanked her.
They went to Pat's and called me.

11. Circle the objective case pronouns.

He threw it toward me.
Pass me the salt.
We made them sandwiches.

12. Circle the reflexive case pronouns and underline the possessive case pronouns.

Carlo was angry, but stopped himself before he said something really mean to his brother.

I was so tired I couldn't force myself to get dressed and join my friends at the mall.

Some people take themselves too seriously and think it's their responsibility to solve everyone else's problems!

13. Circle the demonstrative pronouns and underline the relative pronouns.

That is the most annoying sound that I have ever heard.

Those are the boxes of blankets that Mom plans to take to the SPCA.

Is this the channel that you were watching?

14. Circle the action verbs.

wash	be	hold	cook
would	buy	pray	gnaw
put	write	loan	marry

15. Circle the linking verbs.

appear	took	become	sat
feel	prove	call	grow
study	look	is	lose

16. Circle the regular verbs and underline the irregular verbs.

forgive	grow	buy	walk
wash	hide	sew	put
sit	hear	play	throw

17. Circle the correct form of lay/lie in each sentence.

Joy found her hairbrush (laying, lying) in the suitcase.

The swing has (lain, laid) broken behind the shed for two years.

The boy had (laid, lain) awake before getting up to play.

18. Circle the correct form of sit/set in each sentence.

The class (set, sat) patiently as the teacher took attendance.

Claudia's aunt (sits, sets) the table while Gert cooks dinner.

(Setting, Sitting) on the porch on a cool summer night is the best.

19. Circle the correct tricky verb in each sentence.

Sandy carefully (hanged, hung) her new curtains on the window.

Peter tried to (accept, except) Jim's explanation, but it was difficult.

You (can, may) take another glass of lemonade if you like.

20. Identify the tense of each verb as present, past, future, present perfect, past perfect, future perfect, present progressive, past progressive, or future progressive.

will drive	am driving
had driven	drove
drive	has driven
drives	will have driven

21. Circle the common adjectives in the following sentences.

The pungent aroma of Italian spices filled the busy kitchen of the pizzeria.

Shelley wore a blue dress to the wedding.

We donated our old car to an automotive school where students practice doing repairs.

22. Place the correct indefinite article in front of each noun.

___ house	___ elephant
___ unicorn	___ yellow flower
___ one-way street	___ honor
___ underdog	___ loafer
___ unopened gift	___ orange
___ hour	___ occasion
___ wrist	___ admirer
___ upper level	

23. Circle the proper adjectives.

Italian	Californian	New York
Texan	China	Moroccan
Africa	Japanese	Danish

24. Determine whether the boldfaced word in each sentence is a possessive pronoun or a possessive adjective.

> **His** sneakers were worn, so he bought new ones.
>
> Marissa crossed **her** fingers and hoped the winning ticket would be **hers**.
>
> **My** uncle showed me an autographed Babe Ruth baseball card and said it would one day be mine.

25. Determine whether the boldfaced word in each sentence is a demonstrative pronoun or a demonstrative adjective.

> **This** is really over the top!
>
> Take **this** money and buy yourself a treat.
>
> Watch **these** carefully while they boil.

26. Determine which form of comparative or superlative adjective best completes each sentence.

> Terry's (most high, highest) jump in the high jump was four feet, six inches.
>
> Sean's bank account was (larger, more large) than mine.
>
> Barbara was (best, better) at chess than her roommate Natalie.

27. Circle the correct form of the comparative and superlative adverbs in the following sentences.

> Joel was (less, least) active during the winter than during the summer.
>
> The store brand's price was the (low, lower, lowest) of the three brands.
>
> This was the (long, longer, longest) day of the year.

28. Determine whether the boldfaced word in the sentence is an adjective or an adverb.

> The accounting department ran at a **fast** but friendly pace.
>
> Cory worked **hard** on improving his tennis swing for the tournament.
>
> Nora was sent **straight** to her room for disobeying her parents.

29. Identify the prepositional phrases in the following sentences.

> Ferdinand Magellan was the first explorer to sail around the world.
>
> Without a doubt, regular exercise is necessary for good health.
>
> The little monkey ran around Mom's living room and climbed up the drapes.

30. Determine whether the boldfaced word is a preposition or an adverb.

> Holly was **beside** herself with fear when the child darted into the street.
>
> If we can reach Hightstown **by** five, we may be able to see the president's motorcade go **by**.
>
> Use caution when you walk **across** busy streets.

31. Rewrite each sentence so that the misplaced modifiers are properly placed.

> The woman was walking her dog with hair curlers.
>
> Walking along the shore the sand burned my feet.
>
> Tina bought a guinea pig for her brother they call Butterscotch.

32. Using the clues, write the homonyms, homo-phones, or homographs.

    finished/tossed

    trade event/equitable

    the total/several

    shut/nearby

    dispatched/perfume

    dress in/a good for sale

33. Identify the simple subjects in the following sentences.

    Next week, Scott and Jennifer will get married.

    Shopping sprees can be fun, but very expensive.

    It may be too soon to tell.

34. Identify the simple predicates in the following sentences.

    Reading is good exercise for the brain.

    Try again.

    The log, when turned over, revealed a whole different world.

35. Identify whether each boldfaced word in the following sentences is a direct or an indirect object.

    Brandy took the **pot** of flowers and brought **it** into the garden window.

    Grumbling to himself, Stan dragged the heavy **garbage cans** out to the street.

    He gave **her** a **high five** to assure her that all was well.

36. Identify the verb that correctly agrees with the subject in each sentence.

    Patty (fly, flies) frequently for work.

    All of us (watch, watches) out for one another.

    Nobody (want, wants) to play croquet in the the backyard with me.

37. Identify the verb that correctly completes the following sentences.

    Neither Jessica nor Marty (like, likes) to do the laundry.

    Spaghetti and meatballs (is, are) my favorite Italian meal.

    Sally or Zach (is, are) probably going to be the valedictorian this year.

38. Circle the verb that agrees with the indefinite pronoun in each sentence.

    Everyone (need, needs) to get any homework I assign in on time!

    I hope somebody (taste, tastes) this lasagna before I serve it to see if it's okay.

    Many (stop, stops) by my office to get direc-tions to your cubicle.

39. Determine which pronoun best fits for proper pronoun-antecedent agreement in each sen-tence.

    The boys took _____ time walking home from school.

    Nobody saw _____ name on the cast list.

    The scared joey hopped to _____ mother for security.

40. Identify the adjective and adverb phrases in the following sentences.

    Books with weak spines need to be rein-forced to lengthen their shelf life.

    The lizard scurried across the sidewalk and disappeared into the bushes.

    The cashier with the red hair and braces was especially helpful.

41. Identify the participial phrases, infinitive phrases, and gerund phrases in the following sentences.

> Hoping to win the lottery, Harriet bought 50 tickets for tonight's drawing.
>
> To help pass the time, Jake reads a book that he takes along.
>
> Caring for her ailing grandmother is Lori's focus right now.

42. Identify the appositive phrases in the following sentences.

> Ron, a referee and mentor, is a fair-minded and friendly man.
>
> Jeannine works for KTL, a public relations firm in Kansas City.
>
> Molly, my student, has a very fanciful imagination.

43. Determine whether each group of words is an independent or a subordinate clause.

> If it doesn't rain
>
> We plan to go
>
> Take that back
>
> Because I overslept
>
> Cover your mouth
>
> Remember her birthday

44. Identify the adjective clause in each sentence.

> Now I remember the guy whom you described to me yesterday.
>
> The house at the end of the road is where my father grew up.
>
> The room next to the office is where the professors meet.

45. Identify the noun clause in each sentence.

> I can see what you mean.
>
> What Wendy said took everyone by surprise.
>
> How it ends remains to be seen.

46. Identify the adverb clause in each sentence.

> Unless he gets a pay raise, Brad won't be able to buy a new car.
>
> I could get this job done faster if there were not so many distractions!
>
> Although many cats are loners, they still look to humans for food and shelter.

47. Identify the coordinating conjunction(s) and the word or group of words it is connecting in each sentence.

> Logan or Melanie can go to the retreat if they want to.
>
> Karla wanted to visit longer with her friend, but she had a long drive home and it was late.
>
> We signed up for the early class so we could have the rest of the afternoon free.

48. Identify the simple, compound, complex, and compound-complex sentences.
   a. We can go to dinner now or we can go after the concert.
   b. When the judge announced the winner, the audience clapped loudly, and they gave him a standing ovation.
   c. All of the graduates will receive a degree.
   d. If you try harder, you will certainly achieve success.

49. Add punctuation where necessary in the following sentences.

Nathans birthday is May 21 1991 which fell on a Monday this year

Mr Roberts left a message asking me to pick up these items staples printer paper correction fluid and two boxes of pens I guess the supply closet got raided

All of the girls dresses were pink with white eyelet ruffles on the sleeves edges.

50. Correctly place quotation marks, commas, and end marks in the following sentences.

Why do we need to know how to add or subtract fractions anyway Chris asked Mr. Bowen the math teacher

Im glad you came to the beach with me my cousin whispered because without you I couldnt make the most awesome sand castle and win the contest

Answers

1. The common nouns are *chair, joy, supermarket, understanding, toddlers, saucepan, dancing,* and *hostess. Chair, supermarket,* and *saucepan* are all items that are common unless they're referred to by brand names. *Toddlers* and *hostess* describe people, but because they don't use proper names, they are common nouns. (Lesson 1)

2. The abstract nouns are *peace, livelihood, deceit, cheerfulness,* and *patience.* They are all concepts, rather than tangible objects. In contrast, *telephone, jungle, smile, rubber band, test,* and *eyelash* are all objects, places, or physical characteristics that you can visualize easily. (Lesson 1)

3. The proper nouns are *Texas* (a specific state), *Nancy* (a person's first name), *Mr. Klondike* (a person's name), *Mexico City* (a specific city), *IBM* (a company name), *Spiderman* (a character name), and *Mt. Everest* (a specific mountain). (Lesson 1)

4. The correct answers are *halves, oxen, dishes, houses, booths,* and *hippopotamuses. Halves* correctly translates the *f* in *half*—just like with *hoof/hooves.* Words that end with *-sh,* like *dish,* or *-s,* like *hippopotamus,* require the addition of an *-es* ending. *Ox* is an irregular noun, so this is one of the cases where you need to memorize the plural for future use. *House* and *booth* are basic count nouns, so they get the *-s* added. You'll want to get a feel for the irregular nouns like *ox* and how their plurals work. (Lesson 2)

5. The correct answers are *kilowatt-hours, forget-me-nots, follow-ups,* and *sticks-in-the-mud.* For hyphenated compound nouns like these, add the *-s* (or other plural suffixes as appropriate) to the word that changes in number. (Lesson 2)

6. The correct answers are *child's*, *Jody's*, *tooth's*, *cactus's*, *puppies'*, *moms'*, *Jason's*, *women's*, and *dress's*. For a plural word that already ends in *-s*, use a single apostrophe (like *puppies'*). For a plural noun that ends with a consonant other than the plural *-s* (like *women*), add an *-'s*. For singular nouns that end in *-s* (like *Congress* and *cactus*), you still need to add an *-'s*. For proper names (like *Jody* and *Jason*) and common nouns (like *child*) that are singular, use the simple *-'s*. (Lesson 2)

7. The correct answers are *tree/it*, *King Henry/he*, and *Alice/her*. Objects like trees are gender-neutral, and so should always take the pronoun *it*. The title *King* is associated with males, so the correct pronoun would be *he*. While names aren't always foolproof (perhaps your brother and your aunt are both named Terry), names like *Anthony* and *Alice* are heavily associated with males and females, respectively. A *passenger* is a person, and so should be *he* or *she*, rather than *it*. As for the *kangaroo*, animals generally take the pronoun *it* to avoid confusion. (Lesson 3)

8. The correct answers are:

group/it	*fish/they*
each/he or *she*	*fish/it*
both/they	*women/we*

Antecedents like *both* suggest more than one person, so *they* is the appropriate pronoun. Similarly, *each* suggests individual people, so you would go with *he* or *she*. *Women* is plural, so the word needs a plural pronoun. *Fish* is the tricky one—the word can refer to a single fish or to many fish, so both options are correct unless you know for sure how many fish are being discussed. (Lesson 3)

9. The correct answers are *who*, *whose*, *which*, *whom*, and *whomever*. All of these can be used to begin questions. *Who* is coming with us? *Which* do you want? To *whom* should this e-mail be addressed? *Whomever* should we invite to the party? *When* and *where* are adverbs, not pronouns. (Lesson 3)

10. The correct answers are:

$\boxed{I}$ went to his house and saw him.
$\boxed{She}$ brought me an apple and $\boxed{I}$ thanked her.
$\boxed{They}$ went to Pat's and called me.

All of these pronouns are the subjects of their sentences. In the case of the second, compound sentence, you have two subjects: *she* (who performs the action of bringing the apple), and *I* (who performs the action of thanking her). In the first sentence, *him* is a pronoun, but is the object of the sentence, which makes *him* an objective pronoun. Likewise, *her* in the second sentence and *me* in the third are objective pronouns. (Lesson 3)

11. The correct answers are:

He threw $\boxed{it}$ toward $\boxed{me}$.
Pass $\boxed{me}$ the salt.
We made $\boxed{them}$ sandwiches.

In this question, you're looking for the opposite of the pronouns in question 10. The subjects of the sentences are *he* (the person throwing), *you* (the person who will pass the salt), and *we* (the people who made the sandwiches). So the objects are the people/items that will be affected by the actions. The item being thrown (*it*) and the salt are for *me*, and the sandwiches are for *them*. Those are the objects of the sentences, and therefore the objective pronouns. (Lesson 3)

12. The correct answers are:

> *Carlo was angry, but stopped* himself *before he said something really mean to his brother.*
> *I was so tired I couldn't force* myself *to get dressed and join my friends at the mall.*
> *Some people take* themselves *too seriously and think it's their responsibility to solve everyone else's problems!*

Pronouns containing a variation of *-self*, which refers back to a person or object performing an action, are reflexive pronouns. In these sentences, the reflexive pronouns are *himself*, *myself*, and *themselves* (he stops himself, I force myself, they take themselves). The possessive pronouns (*his, my, their*) show to whom the objects belong. The brother is his, not someone else's. The friends at the mall are mine. The responsibility is theirs. (Lesson 3)

13. The correct answers are:

> That *is the most annoying sound that I have ever heard.*
> Those *are the boxes of blankets that Mom plans to take to the SPCA.*
> *Is* this *the channel that you were watching?*

Demonstrative pronouns like *that, those,* and *this* help you specify what is being discussed. Which sound is the most annoying? Which boxes? Which channel? However, *that* can also do double duty as a relative pronoun, helping you describe earlier nouns or pronouns. (Lesson 3)

14. The action verbs are *wash, hold, cook, buy, pray, gnaw, put, write, loan,* and *marry*. These are all verbs that indicate activity. You can wash a car, hold a baby, cook a meal, buy a present, pray a prayer, gnaw a carrot stick, put an object on a table, write a letter, loan some money, and marry your sweetheart. *Be* and *would* are verbs, but they are linking or helping verbs, which indicate a condition or tell you more about the other parts of a sentence—they need additional words to complete a thought. To *be* is a state, not an action. You can't *would*, but you would get to the mall early. (Lesson 4)

15. The linking verbs are *appear, become, feel, prove, grow, look,* and *is*. Linking verbs connect the nouns and adjectives in a sentence. You can't become, but you can become tired. She feels elated. Karen proves adept at geometry. He grows quiet. I look tired. *Took, sat, call, study,* and *lose* are all simple actions that can stand alone. (Lesson 4)

16. The regular verbs are *walk, wash,* and *play*. The irregular verbs are *forgive, grow, buy, hide, sew, put, sit, hear,* and *throw*. Regular verbs follow a standard pattern when used in the past tense (for example, adding an *-ed: walked, washed,* and *played*). Irregular verbs are words that do not follow such a pattern. *Forgive* becomes *forgave, grow* becomes *grew, buy* becomes *bought, hide* becomes *hid, put* remains *put, sit* becomes *sat, hear* becomes *heard,* and *throw* becomes *threw*. Although *sew* adds *-ed* in the past tense, the past participle is *sewn* (irregular). You should start to familiarize yourself with the irregular verbs, and remember how their past tenses work—memorization is the key. (Lesson 5)

17. The correct answers are *lying*, *lain*, and *lain*. When objects have been resting somewhere, as with Joy's hairbrush, go with forms of *lie*. When people/objects are being placed somewhere, go with *lay* and its participles. (Lesson 5)

18. The correct answers are *sat*, *sets*, and *sitting*. To *sit* means to *be seated* or *be situated* in a particular place, as the students are arranged in class, and the narrator is situated on the porch. To set means to place objects, like putting plates and silverware on a table. (Lesson 5)

19. The correct answers are *hung*, *accept*, and *may*. The verb *to hang* is a tricky one—when one is referring to a person going to the gallows for a crime, go with the regular past participle *hanged*. But in most other cases (hanging objects, hanging around, etc.), *to hang* becomes an irregular verb, and you should use *hung*. To *accept* means to approve/agree, while *except* is a preposition or conjunction that means unless. Looking at the context of the sentence, Peter is evaluating Jim's explanation, which makes approve/agree a more likely option. For the last sentence, look at what is being said. Presumably, the person has the ability to take another glass of lemonade. However, *if you like* tells you that the speaker is really giving permission. When it's an issue of permission over ability, go with *may*. (Lesson 5)

20. The correct answers are:
> **will drive:** *future*
> **am driving:** *present progressive*
> **had driven:** *past perfect*
> **drove:** *past*
> **drive:** *present*
> **has driven:** *present perfect*
> **drives:** *present*
> **will have driven:** *future perfect*

Drive is an irregular verb, but you can still figure out the tense based on the words around the verb. *Will* plus the present *drive* lets you know that the driving will happen in the future. The helping verb *am* tells you that *am driving* is the present progressive. The helping verb *had* is your indicator for the past perfect tense. The past tense of *drive* (which you'll learn in Lesson 5) is *drove*. The helping verb *has* plus the past participle *driven* tell you that you're working with the present perfect. *Drive(s)* is the present tense (*I drive to the store every day, she drives to the store every day*). The helping verbs *will have* plus the past participle *driven* indicate that the action will take place (and finish) in the future, which is the future perfect. (Lesson 6)

21. The common adjectives are *pungent*, *busy*, *blue*, *old*, and *automotive*. Common adjectives are descriptors that are not proper names like *Italian* in the first sentence. (Lesson 7)

22. The correct answers are:

a house	*an* elephant
a unicorn	*a* yellow flower
a one-way street	*an* honor
an underdog	*a* loafer
an unopened gift	*an* orange
an hour	*an* occasion
a wrist	*an* admirer
an upper level	

The best way to determine indefinite articles is to sound out the words. Words that start with a vowel sound (like *underdog, honor,* or *elephant*) call for *an.* Words that start with a consonant—or even just sound like they start with a consonant, like the *w* sound of *one*—call for *a.* (Lesson 7)

23. The proper adjectives are:

Italian	*Moroccan*
Californian	*Japanese*
Texan	*Danish*

Also, *New York* is a proper noun that may also function as a proper adjective (e.g., *New York minute*). Proper adjectives are descriptive proper nouns that tell you about another noun. It should be clear that the proper names are describing other words, and aren't just standalone proper nouns. Common suffixes of proper adjectives are *-ian, -ish,* and *-an,* but you should be aware that there are irregular proper adjectives that don't always follow this pattern. As with irregular verbs and nouns, you should try to memorize the exceptions. (Lesson 7)

24. *His* and *her* are possessive adjectives, *hers* is a possessive pronoun, and *my* is a possessive adjective. To help tell the difference, look at what follows the pronoun. If it's a direct noun (like *sneakers, fingers,* and *uncle*), the pronoun is likely to be possessive. (Lesson 7)

25. The correct answers are *demonstrative pronoun, demonstrative adjective,* and *demonstrative pronoun.* Apply the same test as with question 24: what follows the demonstrative word? If it's a noun, then the demonstrative word is an adjective. If not, it's a demonstrative pronoun. (Lesson 7)

26. The correct answers are *highest, larger,* and *better.* When it comes to comparatives and superlatives, adjectives that are one syllable (like *high*) generally take an *-er* ending (for comparatives when only two things are being compared), or an *-est* ending (for superlatives when more than two things are being compared). (Lesson 7)

27. The correct answers are *less, lowest,* and *longest.* If two items are being compared (as with winter and summer in the first sentence), choose the comparative adverb (*less*). When more than two items are being compared (as with the three brands in the second sentence and all of the days of the year in the third sentence), choose the superlative (*lowest, longest*). (Lesson 8)

28. *Fast* is an adjective; *hard* and *straight* are adverbs. To figure out which is which, you need to look at the words being modified. In the first sentence, *fast* describes *pace,* a noun—and this makes it an adjective. In the second sentence, *hard* modifies *worked,* a verb, and in the third sentence, *straight* modifies *sent,* another verb— so in both of these cases, the modifier is an adverb. (Lessons 7 and 8)

29. The prepositional phrases are *around the world*, *without a doubt*, *for good health*, *around Mom's living room*, and *up the drapes*. To find prepositional phrases, you should familiarize yourself with the common prepositions (Lesson 9). Then, when you see one of them in a sentence followed by a noun or noun phrase, you know it's a prepositional phrase. In these sentences, the key words are *around* (followed by the noun *world*), *without* (followed by the noun *doubt*), *for* (followed by the noun *health*), *around* (followed by the noun *living room*), and *up* (followed by the noun *drapes*). (Lesson 9)

30. The correct answers are preposition (*beside herself*), preposition (*by five*), adverb (*go by*), and preposition (*across busy streets*). If the common preposition in the sentence modifies a noun or pronoun (like *herself* in the first sentence, *five* [o'clock] in the second sentence, and *streets* in the third sentence), then it's an official prepositional phrase. If it stands alone and is not followed by a noun, it's an adverb. (Lesson 9)

31. The correct answers are:

> The woman with hair curlers was walking her dog.
>
> The sand burned my feet while I was walking along the shore.
>
> Tina bought a guinea pig they call Butterscotch for her brother.

In the first sentence, you need to make clear that it was the woman (and not her dog!) who was wearing the hair curlers. The second sentence seems to be saying that the sand was walking. In the third sentence, who is called Butterscotch—the guinea pig or Tina's brother? By making sure that modifiers are placed next to the nouns they're modifying, you make the sentence and its meaning much clearer. (Lesson 10)

32. The correct answers are:

through/threw	*close/close*
fair/fair	*sent/scent*
sum/some	*wear/ware*

(Lesson 10)

33. The simple subjects are *Scott and Jennifer*, *shopping sprees*, and *it*. The subject is the person or object that will be performing the action of the sentence. Who will be getting married? *Scott and Jennifer* will. What is fun? *Shopping sprees* are fun. What may be too soon to tell? *It* may be too soon to tell. To help you identify the subject of a sentence, locate the nouns and pronouns, and determine whether they tell you what the sentence is about. (Lesson 11)

34. The simple predicates are *is*, *try*, and *revealed*. The simple predicate is the verb that shows the action in the sentence. (Lesson 11)

35. The correct answers are:

> **pot:** *direct object*
>
> **it:** *direct object*
>
> **garbage cans:** *direct object*
>
> **her:** *indirect object*
>
> **high five:** *direct object*

(Lesson 11)

36. The correct verbs are *flies*, *watch*, and *wants*. Singular nouns (like *Patty* and *nobody*) take singular verbs (*lies* and *wants*, respectively). Plural nouns (like *all of us*) take plural verbs (*watch*). (Lesson 11)

37. The correct verbs are *likes*, *is*, and *is*. These are a bit trickier, because you need to look more closely at the subjects. In the first sentence, you see *Jessica nor Marty*, which appears to be plural—but the *neither* at the beginning of the sentence tells you that the subject is really no one, which is singular. In the second sentence, although the subject seems like two items (*spaghetti and meatballs*), they combine to create one collective dish, which makes it a singular noun. And in the third sentence, although you see two names (*Sally* and *Zach*), they're separated by *or*—which means that the sentence is about just one of them. Sally will be the valedictorian, or Zach will be the valedictorian. Therefore, the verb needs to be singular to agree with the subject. (Lesson 12)

38. The correct verbs are *needs*, *tastes*, and *stop*. Again, you need to look closely at the subject of the sentence (which, in these cases, are indefinite pronouns). *Everyone* is singular, and takes the singular, third-person verb (*needs*). *Somebody* is singular and first-person, which means it takes the singular, first-person verb (*tastes*). *Many* [people] is plural, and requires a plural verb. (Lesson 12)

39. The correct pronouns are *their*, *his or her*, and *its*. In the first sentence, the subject *the boys* is plural and therefore calls for the plural possessive *their*. In the second sentence, the subject *nobody* is singular—but from the context of the sentence, you can't tell whether the people involved are male or female, so you should include both the male and female singular possessives: *his or her*. In the third sentence, the subject is singular, but it is an animal, so the noun takes the neutral possessive pronoun *its*. (Lesson 12)

40. The correct answers are:
    with weak spines: *adjective phrase*
    across the sidewalk: *adverb phrase*
    into the bushes: *adverb phrase*
    with the red hair and braces: *adjective phrase*
To determine whether you're reading an adjective phrase or an adverb phrase, check to see what the prepositional phrase is modifying. In the first sentence, *with weak spines* describes *books* (a noun), so it is an adjective phrase. In the second sentence, *across the sidewalk* describes *scurried* (a verb) and *into the bushes* modifies *disappeared* (a verb), so both are adverb phrases. In the third sentence, *with the red hair and braces* describes the cashier (a noun), so it is an adjective phrase. (Lesson 13)

41. The correct answers are:
    Hoping to win the lottery: *participial phrase*
    To help pass the time: *infinitive phrase*
    Caring for her ailing grandmother: *gerund phrase*
Participial phrases start with a present tense verb or a past tense verb, and act as an adjective. In the first sentence, *hoping to win the lottery* describes Harriet, so it acts as an adjective and is therefore a participial phrase. An infinitive phrase starts with *to* plus a verb. That the second sentence starts with *to* tells you that it's an infinitive phrase. A gerund phrase start with a gerund—an *-ing* verb acting as a noun. In the third sentence, *caring for her ailing grandmother* is functioning as a noun, because it is a single activity. (Lesson 13)

42. The appositive phrases are *a referee and mentor*, *a public relations firm in Kansas City*, and *my student*. An appositive phrase tells you more detail about a noun or pronoun in a sentence. In the first sentence, *a referee and mentor* tells you more about Ron. In the second sentence, *a public relations firm in Kansas City* tells you more about KTL. In the third sentence, *my student* tells you more about Molly. (Lesson 13)

43. The correct answers are:

> *If it doesn't rain: subordinate clause*
> *We plan to go: independent clause*
> *Take that back: independent clause*
> *Because I overslept: subordinate clause*
> *Cover your mouth: independent clause*
> *Remember her birthday: independent clause*

The best way to determine whether something is an independent clause is to see if it can stand as a sentence on its own. If the clause leaves you hanging (*If it doesn't rain . . .* then what? *Because I overslept . . .* what happened?), then it's a subordinate clause that relies on an independent clause to tell you what's going on in the sentence. Independent clauses might not give you the most information (where do we plan to go?), but they do have a clear subject (like *we* or an implied *you*) and a clear predicate (*plan, take, cover, remember*). (Lesson 14)

44. The adjective clauses are *whom you described, where my father grew up,* and *where the professors meet.* Adjective clauses act as adjectives to describe a noun or pronoun. In the first sentence, *whom you described* modifies *the guy.* In the second sentence, *where my father grew up* modifies *house.* In the third sentence, *where the professors meet* modifies *room.* (Lesson 14)

45. The noun clauses are *what you mean, what Wendy said,* and *how it ends.* Noun clauses are groups of words containing a subject and a verb that, together, stand in for a single noun as part of a sentence. In the first sentence, *what you mean* (or, in other words, *your meaning*) acts as the object of the sentence. In the second sentence, *what Wendy said* (meaning *Wendy's statement*) serves as the subject of the sentence. Likewise, in the third sentence, *how it ends* acts as the subject (it's another way of saying *the ending*). (Lesson 14)

46. The adverb clauses are *unless he gets a pay raise, if there were not so many distractions,* and *although many cats are loners.* Adverb clauses are subordinate clauses that answer *where, when, how,* or *why.* In the first sentence, *unless he gets a pay raise* tells you *how* Brad would be able to buy a new car. In the second sentence, *if there were not so many distractions* answers the question of *why* I can't get the job done faster. In the third sentence, *although many cats are loners* tells you more about *how* cats look to humans for food and shelter. (Lesson 14)

47. The correct answers are:

> *or* (connects *Logan* and *Melanie*)
> *but* (connects *Karla wanted to visit longer with her friend* and *she had a long drive home*)
> *and* (connects *she had a long drive home* and *it was late*)
> *so* (connects *we signed up for the early class* and *we could have the rest of the afternoon free*)

The best way to spot coordinating conjunctions is to memorize the acronym FANBOYS (*for, and, nor, but, or, yet, so*). Once you know those, you can find them within sentences and see which elements they connect. (Lesson 15)

48. The correct answers are:
  a. compound
  b. compound-complex
  c. simple
  d. complex

Sentence **a** contains two subjects (*we* and *we*) and two predicates (*can go to dinner now* and *can go after the concert*), so it is a compound sentence. Sentence **b** contains two independent clauses (*the audience clapped loudly* and *they gave him a standing ovation*) and a subordinate clause (*when the judge announced the winner*), which makes it a compound-complex sentence. Sentence **c** has a single subject (*all of the graduates*) and a single predicate (*will receive a degree*), so it is a simple sentence. Sentence **d** has one subordinate clause (*if you try harder*) and one independent clause (*you will certainly achieve success*), so it is a complex sentence. (Lesson 16)

49. The correct answers are:

  Nathan's birthday is May 21, 1991, which fell on a Monday this year.

  Mr. Roberts left a message asking me to pick up these items: staples, printer paper, correction fluid, and two boxes of pens; I guess the supply closet got raided.

  All of the girls' dresses were pink, with white eyelet ruffles on the sleeves' edges.

In the first sentence, the birthday belongs to Nathan, so you need a possessive apostrophe. Dates take a comma after the day and after the year. And you need a comma to separate the independent clause (*Nathan's birthday is May 21, 1991*) from the dependent clause (*which fell on a Monday this year*). In the second sentence, titles (like *Mr.*, *Mrs.*, *Dr.*, etc.) need a period. Lists of items call for a colon, with commas separating the items. The semicolon separates two independent clauses (*Mr. Roberts left a message asking me to pick up these items . . .* and *I guess the supply closet got raided*) that aren't connected by a conjunction. In the third sentence, the dresses belong to the girls and the edges belong to the sleeves, so you need plural possessive apostrophes. You also need a comma separating the main clause and the dependent adjective phrase (*with white eyelet ruffles on the sleeves' edges*). (Lessons 17–20)

50. The correct answers are:

> *"Why do we need to know how to add or subtract fractions anyway?" Chris asked Mr. Bowen, the math teacher.*
>
> *"I'm glad you came to the beach with me," my cousin whispered, "because without you I couldn't make the most awesome sand castle and win the contest!"*

The most essential part of dialogue is the punctuation—without those marks, how would we know who is talking, and what he or she is saying? In the first sentence, *Chris asked* tells you that he or she is the one speaking. The comma after *Mr. Bowen* sets off a phrase describing Mr. Bowen, and there is no indication that *the math teacher* is part of the quotation. In the second sentence, *my cousin whispered* tells you that the quote is interrupted. This nonspoken part of the sentence is set off by commas, and it's important to make sure that both parts of the quote are set off by beginning and ending quotation marks.
(Lessons 17–20)

NOUNS AND PRONOUNS

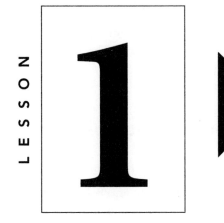

1 ▶ KINDS OF NOUNS

The beginning of wisdom is to call things by their right names.

—Chinese proverb

LESSON SUMMARY

Learn why the noun, and its six identifiable subgroups, is the fundamental component of our language.

Nouns, the most basic component of language, are naming words. They help us identify the persons, places, or things we talk about. There are six distinct groups of nouns: common nouns, proper nouns, concrete nouns, abstract nouns, collective nouns, and compound nouns.

It is important to know about nouns and their function in speaking and writing because so many other parts of speech relate to nouns. So, that is where we will start our grammar refresher. The following page briefly summarizes the six different noun groups and cites the unique qualities that separate them. Then we will look at each individual group in more detail.

The Six Types of Nouns

Common Nouns

A **common noun** is a word that speaks of something only in a general way, like *book*, *car*, and *person*. Common nouns can be written in singular form (*book*, *car*, and *person*) or plural form (*books*, *cars*, and *people*).

Proper Nouns

Unlike common nouns, **proper nouns** name a very specific person, place, or thing. One distinguishing aspect of proper nouns is that they *always* begin with a capital letter. *Catcher in the Rye*, *BMW Z4*, and *Albert Einstein* are proper nouns.

Concrete Nouns

Concrete nouns name something that appeals to your senses. For instance, *toothbrush*, *cell phone*, *moonlight*, *waves*, and *breezes* are all concrete nouns.

Abstract Nouns

In contrast, **abstract nouns** name beliefs, concepts, and characteristics or qualities—things that can't be touched, seen, or accrued. For example, *composure*, *sovereignty*, *free enterprise*, and *daring* are abstract nouns.

Collective Nouns

Collective nouns are words used to name people, places, and things in terms of a unit. For instance, *class*, *flock*, *herd*, and *family* are collective nouns.

Compound Nouns

New words can be formed by combining two or more words, thus creating a compound word. **Compound nouns** can be made up of a number of speech compo-nents, including nouns, verbs, adjectives, and adverbs. Some examples of compound nouns are *motorcycle*, *onlooker*, *input*, and *washing machine*.

Many nouns may fall into more than one of these categories. For example, the noun *school* (of fish) is common, concrete, *and* collective. The noun *well-being* is abstract and compound.

A Closer Look at Nouns

Proper nouns are easily distinguishable from **common nouns** by their capital letters, but be cautious. Don't assume that every word in a sentence that begins with a capital is a proper noun. Basic sentence structure dictates that every sentence must begin with a capital letter—remember that from English class? Also, what might appear to be a proper noun, or some form thereof, could instead be a proper adjective simply because it is describing a noun that follows it in the sentence. For example, the proper noun *Florida* is acting as a proper adjective in the following sentence because it is used to describe the word *sunshine*.

Example:
Almost nothing beats the warmth of Florida sunshine.

In the following sentence, *Florida* is a proper noun because it is not describing another word.

Example:
My family goes to Florida every summer for vacation.

EXAMPLES OF PROPER NOUNS BY CATEGORY	
PEOPLE	
Officials	President Barack Obama, Mayor Diaz, Officer O'Malley
Historic Figures	Benjamin Franklin, Cleopatra, Lewis and Clark
Actors	Audrey Hepburn, Tom Hanks, Lucille Ball
Authors	Jack London, William Shakespeare, O. Henry
Artists	Pablo Picasso, Vincent van Gogh, Georgia O'Keeffe
PLACES	
States	Oklahoma, Michigan, New Jersey
Restaurants	Olive Garden, Red Lobster, Salt Creek Grille
Structures	Eiffel Tower, Washington Monument, Empire State Building
Schools	Penn State University, Central High School, Trinity Elementary
THINGS	
Transportation	Delta Airlines, Greyhound, Amtrak
Businesses	FedEx, Toys "R" Us, Barnes & Noble
Products	Hebrew National hot dogs, Microsoft Word, Pantene shampoo

Practice

Determine whether the boldfaced words are proper nouns or proper adjectives in the following sentences.

1. My sister will never let me forget about the time I got sick on the **Six Flags** roller coaster.

2. His prizewinning essay on the movie *Citizen Kane* helped earn him a scholarship to the film school at **Lincoln University** in **California**.

3. What time do you want to meet before we go to the **Monet** exhibit at the **Metropolitan Museum**?

4. After working at **Dairy Treat** for two summers in a row, **Phil** was tired of ice cream.

5. **Melanie** got up at 5 A.M. every day to do swim laps at the **YMCA** pool.

6. Last week, he made a delicious **Irish** soda bread.

7. The **Irish** celebrate **Saint Patrick's Day** every **March**.

8. **Burger Bistro** is about a mile up **Delancey Street**, but if you see the **Shopper Mart** parking lot, you've gone too far.

9. Would you like to order the **Thai** iced tea with your spring rolls, or would you prefer **French** roast iced coffee instead?

10. Before her vacation to **France**, she wants to brush up on her **French** speaking skills, so she can try to blend in with the **French**.

Concrete nouns are fairly simple to identify. They're nouns that appeal to your senses—hearing, touch, taste, smell, and sight. Besides things like an *avalanche*, a *stretch limo*, *newborn kittens*, or a piping hot plate of *barbeque ribs*, things such as *air*, *cells*, *molecules*, and *atoms* are concrete, even though they can't readily be seen with the naked eye. Got the idea?

Abstract nouns, on the other hand, name ideas, qualities or characteristics, and feelings. Words such as *pride*, *resentfulness*, *health*, *democracy*, and *love* fall into this category. Do you see the difference between the two?

Practice

Identify the boldfaced nouns in the following sentences as either concrete or abstract.

11. Albert shooed the **kids** out of the **kitchen** so he could cook dinner in **peace**.

12. Some see **smartphones** as the **pinnacle** of modern **technology**, but others prefer not to be so plugged in all the time.

13. Her **talent** for **calculus** made her a popular **tutor** for her friends right before a big **test**.

14. The **teacher** hoped he'd be able to get **tenure** after a few more years at his **school**.

15. Because of his **love** for **tennis**, he joined a club at the local **recreation center**, and felt a strong sense of **community** with his fellow players.

Take a look at a list of **collective nouns**, and you're sure to get a few chuckles. Some are fairly familiar, such as *herd*, *club*, *family*, and *committee*. But did you know that a group of oysters is called a *bed*? That a group of butterflies is called a *kaleidoscope*? That a group of islands is called a *chain*? Or that a group of ships is called a *flotilla*?

A collective noun can take either a singular or a plural verb, depending on how it is used in the sentence. Take the word *choir*, for instance, in the following sentence:

The choir travels to out-of-state performances by bus.

Here the *choir* is taken as a single unit and therefore takes the singular verb (*the collective group travels*). The following sentence, on the other hand, uses the word *choir* in a plural sense.

The choir are fitted for new robes every three years.

This implies that all the individual choir members are fitted for new robes. While the sentence may sound odd, this must obviously be the case, as *each* individual member wears a robe; the *group* as a single unit doesn't wear a robe.

Practice

Identify the correct verb or pronoun for each collective noun in the following sentences.

16. My old stamp collection (is, are) collecting dust on my shelf.

17. Mark's parents wanted to give him (its, their) old car for his 16th birthday.

18. The puppies (is, are) exhausted after I took them for a walk.

19. The family agreed to spend (its, their) vacation in Florida next year.

20. Have you heard that the committee finally made (its, their) decision, and will announce it at the next meeting?

TIP

Remember, if a collective noun refers to a whole group, use a singular verb; if the noun refers to the members of the group acting as individuals, use a plural verb. If you're not sure, the general rule is to use the singular. It is almost always acceptable.

Compound nouns can present writers with issues regarding spelling, rather than usage. There are three ways to spell these nouns, which are made up of two or more words. The closed form refers to two words joined without any space between them, such as *bandwagon*, *newspaper*, and *skyscraper*. The open form has a space between multiple words that create one idea, like *water ski* and *stainless steel*. The hyphenated form uses hyphens (-) between the words, like *mother-in-law* and *do-gooder*.

Be careful to distinguish between words that have different meanings as a word pair or as a compound word. The following table lists a few of the most commonly confused compound words.

WORD PAIR	MEANING	COMPOUND WORD	MEANING
all ready	completely prepared	*already*	it happened
all together	as a group	*altogether*	completely
every one	each individual	*everyone*	everybody

TIP

Always check the dictionary to find out if a compound word should be hyphenated, since there are not any hard-and-fast rules. For example, *mini-mart* has a hyphen, while another *mini-compound*, *miniseries*, does not!

Practice

Can you identify the six types of nouns in the following sentences? Identify each boldfaced noun as common, proper, concrete, abstract, collective, or compound. Some nouns may fit into more than one category.

21. With all the crazy **weather** we've been having, it wouldn't surprise me to see a **snowstorm** followed by tropical **temperatures**.

22. For the upcoming **walkathon**, I raised many **dollars** for an **organization**, Doctors Without Borders (**Médecins Sans Frontières** in French).

23. At the **International Food Festival**, we ate Chinese noodles, **banh mi** from **Vietnam**, and Swedish meatballs.

24. Last week, the class visited the Dr. Martin Luther King Jr. **Memorial** in **Washington, D.C.**, and stood in the **place** on the National Mall where he delivered his famous "I Have a Dream" speech.

25. On our first **date**, we found out that we both have a **passion** for skiing, we like the same **TV shows**, and we have two friends in common.

Answers

1. proper adjective (*Six Flags* modifies *roller coaster*)

2. proper noun; proper noun; proper noun

3. proper adjective (*Monet* modifies *exhibit*); proper noun

4. proper noun; proper noun

5. proper noun; proper adjective (*YMCA* modifies *pool*)

6. proper adjective (*Irish* modifies *soda bread*)

7. proper noun; proper noun; proper noun

8. proper noun; proper noun; proper adjective (*Shopper Mart* modifies *parking lot*)

9. proper adjective (*Thai* modifies *iced tea*); proper adjective (*French* modifies *roast*)

10. proper noun; proper adjective (*French* modifies *speaking skills*); proper noun

11. concrete; concrete; abstract

12. concrete; abstract; abstract

13. abstract; abstract; concrete; concrete

14. concrete; abstract; concrete

15. abstract; concrete; concrete; abstract

16. is

17. their

18. are

19. their

20. its

21. **weather:** common, abstract; **snowstorm:** common, concrete, compound; **temperatures:** common, abstract

22. **walkathon:** common, concrete, compound; **dollars:** common, concrete; **organization:** common, concrete, collective; **Médecins Sans Frontières:** proper, concrete, collective

23. **International Food Festival:** proper, concrete; **banh mi:** common, concrete; **Vietnam:** proper, concrete

24. **Memorial:** proper, concrete; **Washington, D.C.:** proper, concrete; **place:** common, concrete

25. **date:** common, concrete; **passion:** common, abstract; **TV shows:** common, concrete

NOUN USAGE

The plural of tragedy is tragedies, but other than Shakespeare's, why would anyone want to go through more than one?

—Mim Granahan, American actor, playwright, director (1972–)

LESSON SUMMARY
Pluralize singular nouns and turn them into possessives with ease—spelling tips included.

Plurals

You can make most, but not all, nouns plural by simply adding *-s* or *-es* to the end of the word, like *printer/printers*, *lunch/lunches*, *bill/bills*, *kiss/kisses*, and *mall/malls*. However, the English language can be tricky. Some nouns change completely as plurals, and others do not change at all. But never fear, there are some rules to help you know how to make a singular noun plural. Read on!

MAKING SINGULAR NOUNS PLURAL

1. Add -s to the end of most nouns to make them plural.
   grill/grills, paper/papers, snake/snakes, razor/razors
   The plural form of nouns like these, referred to as *count nouns*, is rather predictable.

2. Add -es to the end of nouns ending with -ch, -s, -sh, -ss, -x, and -z.
   punch/punches, gas/gases, garlic press/garlic presses, brush/brushes, box/boxes, fez/fezes
   It would be strange to try to pronounce *dresss* or *crashs* if we didn't put an *e* in front of the *s*, which forms another syllable.

3. Change -f, -lf, or -fe at the end of nouns to -ves.
   leaf/leaves, half/halves, knife/knives
   Be careful; there are exceptions to this rule—for example, *chief/chiefs, giraffe/giraffes.*

4. Change -y to -ies when the -y follows a consonant.
   party/parties, battery/batteries, penny/pennies, baby/babies

5. Just add an -s after a -y when the -y is preceded by a vowel.
   guy/guys, day/days, play/plays, key/keys, boy/boys

6. Add -es to nouns ending with an -o that follows a consonant.
   tornado/tornadoes, potato/potatoes, echo/echoes, hero/heroes

7. Simply add -s to nouns ending with an -o that follows another vowel.
   patio/patios, video/videos, radio/radios
   Be careful; there are exceptions to this rule—for example, *banjo/banjos, piano/pianos.*

8. For hyphenated compound nouns, add an -s to the word that is changing in number.
   president-elect/presidents-elect, brother-in-law/brothers-in-law

9. There are no rules for pluralizing irregular nouns; you must memorize them.
   mouse/mice, deer/deer, child/children, man/men, foot/feet, stimulus/stimuli, tooth/teeth, die/dice, louse/lice, ox/oxen

Practice

Decide whether to add *-s* or *-es* to the end of each word in order to make it plural.

1. television

2. roof

3. range

4. hour

5. mess

6. dispatch

7. point

8. blouse

9. inch

10. mesh

Identify the correct plural for each of the boldfaced words.

11. hoof	→	hoofs	hooves
12. winery	→	wineries	winerys
13. season	→	seasones	seasons
14. whim	→	whims	whimes
15. loofah	→	loofahs	loofahes
16. cookie	→	cookys	cookies
17. library	→	libraries	librarys
18. scarf	→	scarfs	scarves
19. party	→	partys	parties
20. donkey	→	donkies	donkeys
21. summary	→	summaries	summarys
22. box	→	boxs	boxes
23. lash	→	lashes	lashs
24. puzzle	→	puzzlees	puzzles
25. bayou	→	bayous	bayoues
26. buzz	→	buzzes	buzzs
27. whiff	→	whives	whiffs
28. life	→	lives	lifes
29. nursery	→	nurserys	nurseries
30. loaf	→	loafs	loaves
31. gloss	→	glosss	glosses

32. alley   →   alleys   allies

33. battery   →   battereys   batteries

34. staff   →   staffs   staves

35. wolf   →   wolfes   wolves

36. movie   →   movies   moviees

37. DVD   →   DVDes   DVDs

38. comedy   →   comedies   comedys

39. blue   →   bluees   blues

40. abyss   →   abysses   abyssies

41. touch   →   touchs   touches

42. mouth   →   mouthes   mouths

43. guppy   →   guppies   guppys

44. dish   →   dishs   dishes

45. prophecy   →   prophecies   prophecys

46. hearth   →   hearthes   hearths

47. status   →   statuss   statuses

48. ox   →   oxes   oxen

49. money   →   moneys   monies

50. carcass   →   carcasses   carcassi

51. mantis   →   manti   mantises

52. lens   →   lenses   lensi

53. bus   →   busses   buses

54. buss	→	busses	buses
55. walrus	→	walruses	walruss
56. iris	→	irisi	irises
57. potato	→	potatoes	potatos
58. axis	→	axises	axes
59. radio	→	radios	radioes
60. studio	→	studioes	studios
61. radius	→	radiuses	radii
62. mosquito	→	mosquitoes	mosquitos
63. mother-in-law	→	mothers-in-law	mother-in-laws
64. seven-year-old	→	sevens-year-old	seven-year-olds
65. cabinetmaker	→	cabinetsmaker	cabinetmakers
66. jack-in-the-box	→	jacks-in-the-box	jack-in-the-boxes
67. president-elect	→	presidents-elect	president-elects
68. seargeant at arms	→	seargeant at arms	seargeants at arms
69. basis	→	basises	bases
70. moose	→	mooses	moose
71. goose	→	geese	gooses
72. crisis	→	criseses	crises
73. erratum	→	errata	erratums
74. veto	→	vetos	vetoes
75. species	→	speciess	species

Possessives

Possessive nouns are words that imply ownership—something belonging to something else. The first thing to do is determine whether the word being used actually implies possession.

Singular Possessives

Look at the sentence *the bird nests had eggs inside*. The word *nests*, while it ends with *-s*, is plural, not possessive. To make *nest* or any singular noun possessive, add an apostrophe and *-s* (*'s*) to the end, as in *child/child's*, *bread/bread's*, or *music/music's*.

> **Example:**
> The *child's* older sister was my *neighbor's friend's* babysitter.

What this sentence tells us is that the older sister of the child was the babysitter of the friend of my neighbor. In other words, the sister "belonged" to the child, the friend "belonged" to the neighbor, and the neighbor "belonged" to me.

Practice

Write the possessive form of the following phrases.

76. the contract of the actor

77. the graduation of Sabrina

78. the price of the car

79. the front door of the house

80. the ball glove of Matt

Plural Possessives

Making a plural noun possessive is a bit different. Most plural nouns end with *-s*, except for irregular nouns (see page 26) like *mouse/mice*, *child/children*, *man/men*, *deer/deer*, and so on. With a regular noun, simply add an apostrophe *after* the *-s* (*s'*), as in *girls/girls'*, *schools/schools'*, or *newspapers/newspapers'*.

> **Example:**
> The *districts' administrators' secretaries'* contracts were approved.

This sentence tells us that the contracts of the secretaries of the administrators of the district were approved. In other words, the administrators "belonged" to the district, the secretaries "belonged" to the administrators, and the contracts "belonged" to the secretaries.

Irregular nouns, such as *teeth* or *feet*, are treated like singular nouns, and *-'s* is added to form their possessives.

> **Example:**
> The *geese's* V formation in the sky was impressive as they flew overhead.

Practice

Write the possessive form of the following phrases.

81. the dictionaries of the writers

82. the calendars of the doctors

83. the hills of ants

84. the islands of the countries

85. the toys of the children

> **TIP**
>
> When you are confronted with a singular noun ending in -s and need to make it possessive, add -'s.
>
> **Examples:**
> **Tess's** new shoes hurt her feet, but she wore them anyway.
> A **cactus's** roots absorb water rapidly.
>
> Certain proper names such as *Jesus*, *Moses*, and *Socrates* are exceptions to this rule. Simply add an apostrophe with no additional *s*.

Plurals Formed with -'s

What's a rule without an exception? There are a few instances where you may need to use apostrophe -*s* (-*'s*) to make a plural. For example, you should add -*'s* to pluralize an abbreviation that has more than one period, such as *Ph.D.* or *M.D.*

> **Example:**
> M.D.'s and Ph.D.'s denote doctorates in medicine and philosophy.

Also, when you need to write an expression with words and letters that usually are not seen in the plural form—like *if*, *and*, or *but*, or *P* and *Q*—add -*'s* to the word or letter.

> **Example:**
> There are no if's, and's, or but's about it; she won't be going to the concert tomorrow. She should have minded her P's and Q's and kept her comments to herself.

> **TIP**
>
> You make some single-letter abbreviations plural by doubling the letter: p (page)/pp (pages), l (line)/ll (lines). Other abbreviations, like units of measure, do not change to become plural: 1 km (kilometer)/10 km (kilometers), 1 in. (inch)/6 in. (inches).

Answers

1. televisions
2. roofs
3. ranges
4. hours
5. messes
6. dispatches
7. points
8. blouses
9. inches
10. meshes
11. hooves
12. wineries
13. seasons
14. whims
15. loofahs
16. cookies
17. libraries
18. scarves
19. parties
20. donkeys
21. summaries
22. boxes
23. lashes
24. puzzles
25. bayous
26. buzzes
27. whiffs
28. lives
29. nurseries
30. loaves
31. glosses
32. alleys
33. batteries
34. staffs
35. wolves
36. movies
37. DVDs
38. comedies
39. blues
40. abysses
41. touches
42. mouths
43. guppies
44. dishes
45. prophecies
46. hearths
47. statuses
48. oxen
49. moneys
50. carcasses
51. mantises
52. lenses
53. buses
54. busses
55. walruses
56. irises
57. potatoes
58. axes
59. radios
60. studios
61. radii
62. mosquitoes
63. mothers-in-law
64. seven-year-olds
65. cabinetmakers
66. jack-in-the-boxes
67. presidents-elect
68. sergeants at arms
69. bases
70. moose
71. geese
72. crises
73. errata
74. vetoes
75. species
76. the actor's contract
77. Sabrina's graduation
78. the car's price

79. the house's front door

80. Matt's ball glove

81. the writers' dictionaries

82. the doctors' calendars

83. the ants' hills

84. the countries' islands

85. the children's toys

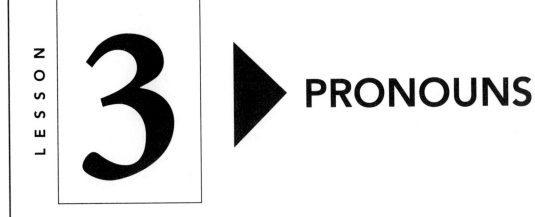

L E S S O N

3 ▶ PRONOUNS

We were always together, and were frequently mistaken for twins. We shared everything, and on my birthday, gifts were bestowed on him too; on his, upon me. Each had forgotten the first person singular of the personal pronoun, and not until comparatively late in life did I learn to use "I" and "me" in the place of "we" and "us."

—Georg Moritz Ebers, German novelist
and Egyptologist (1837–1898)

LESSON SUMMARY

A pronoun is more than "a word that takes the place of a noun." Learn about pronoun categories and cases, and the importance of making them agree in *number*, *gender*, and *person*.

Pronouns take the place of, or refer to, a specific noun in a sentence. To use pronouns correctly, make sure they agree in gender, number, and person with the noun they are replacing or referring to (the antecedent, or referent noun).

Gender

The English language has three genders: masculine, feminine, and neuter. A pronoun's gender tells if it is replacing (or referring to) a masculine, feminine, or neuter noun. To refer to a male, we use *he*, *his*, and *him*; to a female, *she*, *her*, and *hers*; and to animals or things, *it* and *its*.

Examples:
Joseph took Wanda's car to the mechanic.
He took her car to the mechanic.
He took **it** to the mechanic.

In today's society, we are moving away from gender-specific titles and using more inclusive words, such as *police officer*, *firefighter*, *mail carrier*, and *flight attendant*, rather than *policeman*, *fireman*, *mailman*, and *stewardess*. It is never correct, however, to refer to people as *it*, so the pronouns *he* and *she* must still be used when referring to a particular person.

Number

A pronoun that takes the place of or refers to a singular noun (one person, place, or thing) must be singular as well. The same applies to plural pronouns and nouns.

Examples:
If an **employee** wants to park in the hospital parking lot, then **he or she** must apply for the appropriate tag to do so.
Employees who need to renew **their** parking tags must show **their** current hospital ID cards.

Words like *anybody*, *anyone*, *everybody*, *everyone*, *each*, *neither*, *nobody*, and the like are singular and must take a singular pronoun:

Everybody must have **his or her** ID card validated.

To avoid awkward language, it is sometimes better to recast the sentence in the plural:

Employees must have **their** ID cards validated.

Person

English grammar has three "persons": first, second, and third. First-person pronouns like *I*, *me*, *we*, and *us* include the speaker. Second-person pronouns involve only *you*, *your*, and *yours*. Third-person pronouns—*he*, *she*, *it*, *they*, *them*, and so on—include everybody else.

Examples:
I went with **my** family to Yellowstone State Park.
You wouldn't have believed **your** eyes—the scenery was amazing.
Doug said **he** would take photos with **his** new camera.

Categories and Cases

Pronouns are divided into five categories: personal, demonstrative, relative, indefinite, and interrogative, and four cases: subjective, objective, possessive, and reflexive.

Personal Pronouns
Personal pronouns can refer to the speaker or speakers (first person), to those being spoken to (second person), or to those who are spoken about (third person). The following table shows the subjective case personal pronouns, which are pronouns used as the subject of a sentence.

SUBJECTIVE CASE PERSONAL PRONOUNS			
	FIRST PERSON	**SECOND PERSON**	**THIRD PERSON**
Singular	I	you	he, she, it
Plural	we	you	they

In a sentence containing a pronoun, the word the pronoun refers to is called the antecedent.

Example:
Trent is a bricklayer. **He** builds homes and buildings.

The antecedent for the pronoun *he* is *Trent.*

Example:
Lydia took **her** to the bank.

Because there is no antecedent mentioned for the pronoun *her*, this sentence is unclear.

Objective case pronouns are used as objects (receivers of action) in a sentence. (See Lesson 11 for more about objects.) The following table shows the objective case personal pronouns.

OBJECTIVE CASE PERSONAL PRONOUNS		
	FIRST PERSON	**SECOND PERSON**	**THIRD PERSON**
Singular	me	you	him, her, it
Plural	us	you	them

The following sentences show how objective case pronouns are used.

Please give **me** the envelope to put in the mailbox.

Should I send **him** to boarding school this year? I gave **you** flowers for graduation, remember?

Personal pronouns can also show possession—to whom something belongs. The following table shows the possessive case personal pronouns.

POSSESSIVE CASE PERSONAL PRONOUNS		
	FIRST PERSON	**SECOND PERSON**	**THIRD PERSON**
Singular	my, mine	your, yours	his, her, hers, its
Plural	our, ours	your, yours	their, theirs

The following sentences show how possessive case pronouns are used.

This old gray house is **mine**; the new white one over there is **his**.
Hers, around the corner, is getting **its** roof replaced. **My** roof probably needs replacing soon. **Our** neighbors are getting **their** driveway repaved.

TIP

Remember, *your* is a possessive pronoun and *you're* is a contraction meaning "you are." Try not to confuse the two in *your* e-mails or other things *you're* writing!

Lastly, reflexive case pronouns, sometimes called *selfish* pronouns, are used to show a subject performing some kind of action upon itself. Reflexive pronouns can act only as objects in a sentence, never as subjects. The following table shows the reflexive case personal pronouns.

REFLEXIVE CASE PERSONAL PRONOUNS			
	FIRST PERSON	**SECOND PERSON**	**THIRD PERSON**
Singular	myself	yourself	himself, herself, itself
Plural	ourselves	yourselves	themselves

The following sentences show how reflexive pronouns are used. Notice that they are used only as objects.

> He cut **himself** on the edge of the can while opening it.
> It was obvious they thought of **themselves** as experts.
> The computerized car drove **itself** during the demonstration.

Practice

Identify the case of the boldfaced pronouns in each of the sentences.

1. Andrew couldn't remember where **he** had left **his** economics textbook.

2. Do you want to try the new Mexican restaurant, or the burger place **we** talked about last week?

3. Maria's group had trouble working together on the project because **they** all wanted to use **their** own ideas.

4. I offered to help Jerry shop for **his** party, but **he** said he could handle **it himself**.

5. Before Melissa could save the document **she** was working on, **her** computer crashed and restarted **itself**.

6. As a child, Chris had acted in commercials, but **it** was something **he** preferred to keep to **himself** as an adult.

7. The ice cream parlor was out of Alana's favorite flavor, so **she** had to pick a different one to replace **it**.

8. Elton couldn't remember if **he** had locked the doors, so **he** went downstairs to check **them**.

9. **She** fed the ducks at the pond so regularly that **they** would walk up and take the pieces of bread right from **her**.

10. **Their** kids are much older now than **they** appear in the photos—**they** have outgrown **their** toothless smiles.

Demonstrative Pronouns

The four **demonstrative pronouns**—*this, that, these,* and *those*—refer to things in relation to number and distance. These pronouns can act as a subject or an object.

DEMONSTRATIVE PRONOUNS		
	SINGULAR	**PLURAL**
Near	this	these
Far	that	those

Demonstrative pronouns look like this in sentences:

> **This** tastes awful, Mom!
> I should take **these** and give them to Shelly.
> **Those** are his, not yours.
> I want **that** for my collection.

Relative Pronouns

The **relative pronouns**—*that, which, who,* and *whom*—relate (or refer back) to another noun that precedes the pronoun in the sentence and introduce clauses that describe earlier nouns or pronouns.

> **Examples:**
> I own the boat **that** won the race.
> The man **who** drove it is my best friend, Jack.
> He is someone on **whom** I rely for skill and expertise.
> We have entered into the next race, **which** is on Friday.

Notice that *who* and *whom* refer to a person, while *which* and *that* refer to things. Use *that* to signify information that is necessary (restrictive) to the meaning of the sentence, and *which* to signify information that is discretionary (nonrestrictive), in that even if it is removed, the meaning of the sentence is not altered.

> **TIP**
>
> Here's an easy way to remember whether to use *who* or *whom*: use who when you'd use *she* or *he* and *whom* when you'd use *her* or *him*. Examples: *Who* is calling? *She* is. To *whom* should I give the letter? To *him*!

Indefinite Pronouns

Indefinite pronouns refer to unspecified people, places, or things. Some indefinite pronouns are always singular, some are always plural, and others can be both, depending on what or whom they're referring to. See the following table for the classifications.

INDEFINITE PRONOUNS				
SINGULAR			**PLURAL**	**BOTH**
another	anyone	no one	both	all
anybody	anything	nobody	few	most
everyone	everybody	one	many	none
everything	nothing	someone	several	some
each	either	somebody		
something				

Here are some examples of how indefinite pronouns are used in sentences.

> **Both** of the families took their daughters camping in Jackson Hole, Wyoming.
> **Each** of the girls brought her journal with her.
> **All** of the campers are expected to keep their sites litter-free.

Interrogative Pronouns

Interrogative pronouns are pronouns that begin questions: *who, whom, whose, which,* and *what.*

> **Examples:**
> **Who** put the milk in the freezer?
> **What** is the sum of 12 and 31?
> To **whom** does this black jacket belong?
> **Which** is the road to Spring Lake?
> **Whose** is that pen on the floor over there?

When these pronouns are not acting as interrogative pronouns, they also play the roles of relative and personal pronouns in sentences.

Practice

Determine whether the boldfaced pronoun is *demonstrative*, *relative*, *indefinite*, or *interrogative*.

11. **That** was the first **one** to arrive.

12. **This** is the best homemade lasagna I have ever had.

13. The plants **that** I bought yesterday require full sunlight during the day.

14. **Who** wants to go to the farmer's market with me tomorrow?

15. Georgia is the only **one** in the car who noticed that we had taken a wrong turn on Foster Street.

16. **No one** volunteered to make any batches of brownies for the elementary school bake sale, so I volunteered to make **several**.

17. "**Which** of the ties should I wear to the ceremony?" Bob asked out loud, even though **no one** was in the room.

18. Pam thought **that** was the nicest table at the store, but Phil preferred the glass-topped **one**.

19. **What** did he say when he read the article?

20. **These** are $25 **each**.

Answers

1. **he:** subjective; **his:** possessive
2. **we:** subjective
3. **they:** subjective; **their:** possessive
4. **his:** possessive; **he:** subjective; **it:** objective; **himself:** reflexive
5. **she:** subjective; **her:** possessive; **itself:** reflexive
6. **it:** subjective; **he:** subjective; **himself:** reflexive
7. **she:** subjective; **it:** objective
8. **he:** subjective; **he:** subjective; **them:** objective
9. **she:** subjective; **they:** subjective; **her:** objective
10. **their:** possessive; **they:** subjective; **they:** subjective; **their:** possessive
11. **that:** demonstrative; **one:** indefinite
12. **this:** demonstrative
13. **that:** relative
14. **who:** interrogative
15. **one:** indefinite
16. **no one:** indefinite; **several:** indefinite
17. **which:** interrogative; **no one:** indefinite
18. **that:** demonstrative; **one:** indefinite
19. **what:** interrogative
20. **these:** demonstrative; **each:** indefinite

VERBS

LESSON

4 ▶ VERB TYPES

After the verb "to love," "to help" is the most beautiful verb in the world.

—Bertha von Suttner, Austrian writer, pacifist, and first woman to win the Nobel Peace Prize (1843–1914)

LESSON SUMMARY
Some action and linking verbs look the same. Learn how to tell the difference, and get some help with helping verbs along the way.

Verbs are "doing" words that are a necessary part of any sentence. This chapter covers three types of verbs: action verbs, linking verbs, and helping verbs. As you can tell, they all "do" something!

Action Verbs

Most **action verbs** represent a visible action, one that can be seen with our eyes. For example, *waltz, surf, gallop, chop, row, swing,* and *punch* are action verbs.

Identifying such *doing words* in a sentence is generally easy. But some action verbs are more difficult to identify because the action is far less obvious, as in *depend, yearn, foresee, understand, consider, require, mean, remember,* and *suppose.* It is helpful to remember that *mental* verbs are action verbs too, even though they are less visible than the others.

Practice

Identify the action verbs in the following sentences.

1. She volunteers twice a week at the local home-less shelter, where she hands out blankets and warm meals for the people who come in.

2. The dog jumped several feet off the ground and caught the stick in its mouth, before running back to its owner.

3. He understood the directions, but took extra time with the test questions to make sure he answered the questions fully.

4. I suppose we should celebrate our anniversary at the restaurant where we had our first date.

5. They danced for hours, took a short break, and then headed back out to the dance floor.

6. His breath fogged the windows in the cold weather, making it difficult for him to see out-side the car.

7. Although Sue gave very clear directions about what kind of haircut she wanted, the hair-dresser cut her hair too short.

8. She saw that movie three times in the theater, and considered it one of her favorites.

9. Mario spent his birthday playing paintball with his friends and eating pizza afterward.

10. After I drove halfway to work, I remembered that I had left my lunch on the counter at home.

Linking Verbs

Unlike the action verb, the **linking verb** expresses a state of being or a condition. Specifically, it links, or connects, a noun with an adjective (a descriptor) or another noun (an identifier) in a sentence.

Example:
Nathan and Sara **are** hardworking students.

The noun **students** identifies or renames the compound subjects, *Nathan and Sara*; *hardworking* is an adjective describing the noun *students*; and the verb *are* links the two components together.

Example:
Collin **was** tired after his golf game.

The adjective *tired* describes the subject, Collin, and the verb *was* links the two components together.

Some linking verbs can be tricky to identify because they appear to be action verbs. Their job in the sentence is to clarify the condition or state of the noun to which they are connected. The verbs in the following list can act not only as action verbs, but also as linking verbs.

appear	become	feel	grow	look
prove	remain	seem	smell	sound
stay	taste	come	lie	prove
act	turn	fall	get	

How can one tell which role these tricky verbs are playing? Let's take a look at the word *turned*, used in two different ways.

The Ferris wheel **turned** slowly as it began its initial rotation.

Here, the Ferris wheel performed an action: It *turned*. Can you visualize the huge wheel slowly rotating, with the riders in the cars, as it warms up? The word *turned* here is an action verb. Let's look at another example:

One frightened rider **turned** green as the ride began to speed up quickly.

Here, the word *turned* connects the describing word, or adjective—*green*—to the subject—*rider*. In this example, *turned* is acting as a linking verb, not an action verb.

LINKING VERBS							
am	is	are	was	were	be	being	been

One easy way to tell whether a verb is an action verb or a linking verb is to replace the verb in question with a verb form of *be* (from the preceding table), or a linking verb like *seemed* or *became*. If the new sentence still makes sense, then you have a linking verb. If the sentence loses its meaning, then you have an action verb. For instance:

The farmer **grew** several prize-winning tomatoes this season.

Let's replace *grew* with *is*:

The farmer **is** several prize-winning tomatoes this season.

Or, let's use the word *seemed*:

The farmer **seemed** several prize-winning tomatoes this season.

Neither choice works, which means that *grew* is an action verb, not a linking verb, in this sentence.

Let's try another example.

The beef stew we had for dinner **tasted** delicious.

This time, let's replace *tasted* with *was*:

The beef stew we had for dinner **was** delicious.

Or, let's use the word *looked*:

The beef stew we had for dinner **looked** delicious.

Both choices make sense because in this sentence *tasted* is a linking verb, not an action verb.

Practice
Determine whether the boldfaced verbs in the following sentences are action or linking verbs.

11. She **appeared** thrilled at the news, even though the promotion would mean more work for her to do.

12. Jenna **appeared** from nowhere—I didn't even hear her come in!

13. The baking cookies **smelled** amazing.

14. Antonia **smelled** bacon frying, and knew that her dad was downstairs making a big breakfast for the family.

15. Brian **became** panicked when he looked at the clock and realized that he was running out of time to finish his math test.

16. Malik **supposed** that Ellie would meet him at the mall after she finished up her chores.

17. The prosecutor **announced** that the defendant had lied about his whereabouts on the night of the crime.

18. We **were** about to leave for the movies last night when we discovered that the car battery had died.

19. She **was** so sure that she had the winning lottery number, so she was disappointed when she lost after all.

20. "I **am** on the way," he texted me.

Helping Verbs

Helping verbs enhance the main verb's meaning by providing more information about its tense.

A main verb may have as many as three helping verbs in front of it in a sentence.

Examples:
Martin **walked** quickly to the bus stop to avoid being late.
Martin **had walked** quickly to the bus stop to avoid being late.
Martin **must have walked** quickly to the bus stop to avoid being late.

A main verb with helping verbs is called a **verb phrase**. It is important to remember that a helping verb need not be right next to the main verb in the sentence. For instance, we could rewrite the last sentence so that the adverb *quickly* separates the helping verbs *must* and *have* from the main verb *walked*.

Example:
Martin **must have** quickly **walked** to the bus stop to avoid being late.

If you were asked to identify the verb phrase, you would eliminate the adverb *quickly* and give *must have walked* as the answer.

The range of a verb phrase is defined as both "the main verb plus its auxiliaries," as previously explained, and "the main verb plus its auxiliaries, its complements, and other modifiers." So some instructors might expect you to identify the previous verb phrase as *must have walked quickly to the bus stop.*

Practice
Identify the verb phrases in the following sentences.

21. If we had known it would rain, we would have packed umbrellas.

22. In March, Esther will have spent 35 years working at this company.

23. We should have left the house about an hour earlier if we wanted to get to the airport on time.

24. Gary had been mowing the lawn, but stopped when Bill came by to chat.

25. For the school fundraiser, Angie is making her famous coconut cupcakes, which will be top sellers.

COMMON HELPING VERBS								
am	is	are	was	were	be	do	does	did
have	had	has	may	might	must	shall	will	can
	should	would	could	ought				

Answers

1. volunteers; hands; come
2. jumped; caught; running
3. understood; took; answered
4. suppose; celebrate; had
5. danced; took; headed
6. fogged, making; see
7. gave; wanted; cut
8. saw; considered
9. spent; playing; eating
10. drove; remembered; left
11. linking
12. action
13. linking
14. action
15. linking
16. action
17. action
18. linking
19. linking
20. linking
21. had known; would have packed
22. will have spent
23. should have left
24. had been mowing
25. is making; will be

LESSON

5 ▶ REGULAR AND IRREGULAR VERBS

They've a temper, some of them—particularly verbs: they're the proudest—adjectives you can do anything with, but not verbs—however, I can manage the whole lot of them!

—Lewis Carroll, British author, mathematician, and clergyman (1832–1898)

LESSON SUMMARY
Become better acquainted with the pesky past-tense verbs that do not end with *-ed,* and learn about proper usage with tricky verbs such as *lay/lie* and *sit/set.*

ost, but not all, verbs follow a simple and predictable pattern when expressing past action. These verbs, called **regular verbs**, can be changed from the present tense to the past tense by simply adding *-ed* or *-d.*

Example:
Those musicians **play** jazz well. But last evening, they surprised the crowd and **played** some blues.

Irregular verbs, on the other hand, do not follow any pattern when forming the past tense, so they require memorization.

Example:
"**Put** the tennis racquets away in the storage bin, please," said Coach. "I **put** them away already," replied Kevin.

Here, the irregular verb *put* stays the same whether it is past or present. Some other verbs that follow suit are *cost, burst, bid, cut,* and *set.*

On the following pages, you'll find a list of common irregular verbs.

COMMON IRREGULAR VERBS

PRESENT	PAST	PAST PARTICIPLE
be	was/were	been
beat	beat	beaten
become	became	become
begin	began	begun
bite	bit	bitten
blow	blew	blown
break	broke	broken
bring	brought	brought
broadcast	broadcast	broadcast
build	built	built
buy	bought	bought
catch	caught	caught
choose	chose	chosen
come	came	come
cost	cost	cost
cut	cut	cut
do	did	done
draw	drew	drawn
drink	drank	drunk
drive	drove	driven
eat	ate	eaten
fall	fell	fallen
feed	fed	fed
feel	felt	felt
fight	fought	fought
find	found	found
fly	flew	flown

COMMON IRREGULAR VERBS (continued)

PRESENT	PAST	PAST PARTICIPLE
forbid	forbade	forbidden
forget	forgot	forgotten
forgive	forgave	forgiven
freeze	froze	frozen
get	got	gotten
give	gave	given
go	went	gone
grow	grew	grown
hang	hung	hung
have	had	had
hear	heard	heard
hide	hid	hidden
hit	hit	hit
hold	held	held
hurt	hurt	hurt
keep	kept	kept
know	knew	known
lay	laid	laid
lead	led	led
learn	learned/learnt	learned/learnt
leave	left	left
lend	lent	lent
let	let	let
lie	lay	lain
light	lit	lit
lose	lost	lost
make	made	made

COMMON IRREGULAR VERBS *(continued)*		
PRESENT	**PAST**	**PAST PARTICIPLE**
mean	meant	meant
meet	met	met
mistake	mistook	mistaken
mow	mowed	mowed/mown
pay	paid	paid
proofread	proofread	proofread
put	put	put
quit	quit	quit
read	read	read
ride	rode	ridden
ring	rang	rung
rise	rose	risen
run	ran	run
say	said	said
see	saw	seen
seek	sought	sought
sell	sold	sold
send	sent	sent
sew	sewed	sewed/sewn
shake	shook	shaken
shave	shaved	shaved/shaven
shine	shone	shone
shoot	shot	shot
show	showed	showed/shown
shrink	shrank	shrunk
shut	shut	shut

COMMON IRREGULAR VERBS (continued)

PRESENT	PAST	PAST PARTICIPLE
sing	sang	sung
sink	sank	sunk
sit	sat	sat
sleep	slept	slept
slide	slid	slid
speak	spoke	spoken
speed	speeded/sped	speeded/sped
spend	spent	spent
spread	spread	spread
spring	sprang	sprung
stand	stood	stood
steal	stole	stolen
stick	stuck	stuck
sting	stung	stung
strike	struck	struck/stricken
strive	strove/strived	striven/strived
swear	swore	sworn
swim	swam	swum
take	took	taken
teach	taught	taught
tear	tore	torn
tell	told	told
think	thought	thought
throw	threw	thrown
understand	understood	understood
upset	upset	upset

COMMON IRREGULAR VERBS *(continued)*		
PRESENT	PAST	PAST PARTICIPLE
wake	woke	woken
wear	wore	worn
weep	wept	wept
win	won	won
wind	wound	wound
write	wrote	written

TIP

If this list seems way too long to memorize, try memorizing three or four words a day and using them somewhere in conversation during the next 24-hour period!

Practice

Determine whether the boldfaced verb in the sentence is correct. Make any necessary corrections.

1. She **is making** a mess when she did her art project last night.

2. In Spanish class this week, we **are conjugated** irregular verbs.

3. The power **went out** right in the middle of my favorite show.

4. Because she disagreed with the committee's decision, the president **vetoed** the new proposal.

5. Rudy let me borrow his bicycle pump, so tomorrow I **had fixed** my flat tire.

6. After the football game, I **had lose** my voice because I cheered so much.

7. When he called me "Karen," I realized he **was mistook** me for someone else.

8. He bragged so much about winning the board game that none of us **will been** in a hurry to play with him again.

9. The cat **dozing** on the sunniest spot on the floor for hours.

10. The party **broke up** after the neighbors complained about the noise and loud music.

Problem Verbs

Conjugating irregular verbs can be a bit challenging. But there are two pairs of irregular verbs that present an additional challenge because they sound alike, even though they do not mean the same thing: *lay/lie* and *set/sit*.

LAY OR LIE			
PRESENT	**PRESENT PARTICIPLE**	**PAST**	**PAST PARTICIPLE**
lay, lays	(am, is, are, was) **laying**	**laid**	(have, has) **laid**

To *lay* means to *place or put* an object somewhere. This object, a noun, must always follow the verb *lay*, making that noun what we call a direct object—the object that directly receives the action from the verb it follows.

Example:
Martin **laid** the blanket on the grass before **laying** the basket of delicious food on it.

PRESENT	**PRESENT PARTICIPLE**	**PAST**	**PAST PARTICIPLE**
lie, lies	(am, is, are, was) **lying**	**lay**	(have, has) **lain**

To *lie* means to *rest or recline* or to *be positioned*. Instead of a noun, a prepositional phrase or an adverb usually follows the verb to complete the sentence or thought.

Example:
The large old oak tree **lies** at the edge of the field. The cattle **have lain** in its shade for over a century.

In these sentences, the prepositional phrases *at the edge, of the field, in its shade,* and *for over a century* clarify the writer's thought.

TIP

Lie/lay are intransitive verbs—they don't need to act on anything. You *lie* down now, or you *lay* down last night. Just you. But *lay/laid* are transitive verbs—they need some object to manipulate. You can *lay* a <u>blanket</u> on the bed—in fact, last night you *laid* one there!

Practice

In each sentence, select the correct form of the verb *lay* or *lie.*

11. When the head of state died, his body was to (lay, lie) in state for a week.

12. After spilling juice all over the floor, Justin (laid, lain) paper towels over the mess.

13. Sick with the flu, all Tracy could do was (lay, lie) still on the couch, dozing and watching television.

14. The neighbors are arguing over the giant maple tree that (lays, lies) on the line that divides their properties.

15. That pile of books has (lain, laid) there for weeks—when do you plan to put them away?

SET OR SIT			
PRESENT	**PRESENT PARTICIPLE**	**PAST**	**PAST PARTICIPLE**
set, sets	(am, is, are, was) **setting**	set	(have, has) **set**

To *set* means to *place or put* an object somewhere. Like the verb *lay*, it must be followed by a noun.

Example:

A harried young mother **sets** her groceries on the counter and tends to her crying son. She **has set** a pillow on the sofa for his nap.

PRESENT	**PRESENT PARTICIPLE**	**PAST**	**PAST PARTICIPLE**
sit, sits	(am, is, are, was) **sitting**	sat	(have, has) **sat**

To *sit* means to *be situated* or to *be seated or resting*. Like the verb *lie*, it is usually followed by a prepositional phrase or an adverb for further clarification.

Example:

I usually **sit** in the front row of the theater for an unobstructed view of the performance.

When I **have sat** further back, I have found that I could not see the actors well.

Practice

In each sentence, select the correct form of the verb *set* or *sit*.

16. We (set, sat) on the beach for hours, talking and watching the waves roll in and out.

17. We (set, sat) our chairs on the beach, along with the umbrella and cooler.

18. She was (sitting, setting) in the third row, but the room was so packed that I couldn't even see her in the crowd.

19. "Would you mind (sitting, setting) my glass on the table for me?" Girard asked.

20. Those stone lion statues have been (setting, sitting) outside the New York Public Library since 1911.

Other Tricky Verbs

Several other verbs need special attention in order to be used correctly.

Most likely, *accept* and *except* are often misused because they sound somewhat alike. Their meanings, however, are very different. To *accept* means to *approve*, *agree*, or *willingly receive*, whereas *except* is really a preposition or conjunction that means *excluding* or *unless*.

Example:

I would **accept** your apology for being late today, but **except** for yesterday, you have been late every day this week.

If you're still confused about whether to *except* or *accept*, remember that when you agree to, or *accept*, something, you are "**CC**-ing" eye-to-eye with someone; when you make an *exception*, you are "**X**-cluding" something in that agreement.

Another pair of verbs often confused in ordinary speech is *can* and *may*.

Can means having the ability to do something. When you say *Can I help you?* what you're really asking is whether you *have the ability* to help this person. (Unless you're completely indisposed in some way, the question leads one to wonder why you would ask it in the first place!)

May, on the other hand, means having permission to do something. When you say *May I help you?* you are asking someone to *allow* you to help him or her.

Example:
I **can** help you rake leaves this afternoon only after I finish my other chores. **May** I help you with it tomorrow instead?

The verbs *hang* and *lie* are unusual because they can be either regular or irregular, depending on their meaning in a sentence. If *hang* refers to a thief going to the gallows, then it is a regular verb and is conjugated *hang, hanged, hanged*. But if it is used in the sense of hanging out with friends or hanging a picture on the wall, then it is an irregular verb and is conjugated *hang, hung, hung*. Similarly, when *lie* means telling an untruth, it's a regular verb, conjugated *lie, lied, lied*. When it means to recline, it is an irregular verb, which we conjugated earlier in this lesson.

Practice

In each sentence, select the correct verb to complete the sentence.

21. (Can, May) I offer you a cup of coffee before you go?

22. It took us two hours, but we (hung, hanged) all of the ornaments on the Christmas tree.

23. In the Old West, criminals were often (hung, hanged) for severe crimes.

24. He was finally able to (accept, except) that they weren't going to have enough time to see the Empire State Building before they left New York City.

25. Everything in my closet seemed to be in order, (accept, except) my favorite pair of sneakers, which were nowhere to be found.

Answers

1. incorrect; **made**
2. incorrect; **are conjugating**
3. correct
4. correct
5. incorrect; **will fix**
6. incorrect; **had lost**
7. incorrect; **was mistaking**, **had mistaken**, or **mistook**
8. incorrect; **will be**
9. incorrect; **dozed** or **has been dozing**
10. correct
11. lie
12. laid
13. lie
14. lies
15. lain
16. sat
17. set
18. sitting
19. setting
20. sitting
21. may
22. hung
23. hanged
24. accept
25. except

6 ▶ VERB FORMS AND TENSES

The future is an unknown, but a somewhat predictable unknown. To look to the future we must first look back upon the past. That is where the seeds of the future were planted. I never think of the future. It comes soon enough.

—Albert Einstein, German-born American scientist and recipient of the 1921 Nobel Prize in Physics (1879–1955)

LESSON SUMMARY

Since every sentence needs a verb, it is essential to have a basic understanding of the four verb forms so that you can use verb tenses properly. This lesson covers not only the four forms, but also verb tenses from basic to perfect to progressive!

When we speak and write, verb tenses help our listeners and readers understand when something is happening. The tricky thing is to remember to be consistent with your verb tenses so your audience does not get confused. In order to use verb tenses properly, we need to really understand the differences between the four basic verb forms of the English language.

Verb Forms

Verb forms may look similar to tenses, but they are not. Learning the following basic forms, or principal parts, will help you use correct verb tenses later in this lesson.

Present

The **present** form of a verb is usually the first entry you find in a dictionary (e.g., *care, forgive, think,* etc.). Sometimes an *-s* is added to the end of the present form of the verb when it is used in conjunction with a singular noun: *she cares, he forgives, it thinks.*

Present Participle

The **present participle** is made by adding the suffix *-ing* to the present form; it is always accompanied by a *be* verb (see Lesson 5), which acts as a helping verb, forming what is called a **verb phrase**: *am caring, is forgiving, were thinking.* Notice that this verb form expresses action that is ongoing.

Past

The **past** form of a verb shows action or existence that has already taken place at a point in time before now (e.g., *she cared, they forgave, he thought*). Remember that all regular verbs end in *-ed* in the past tense, whereas irregular verbs end in a variety of ways.

Past Participle

The **past participle** of a verb consists of its past form, accompanied by the helping verb *have, has,* or *had* (e.g., *have cared, has forgiven, had thought,* etc.). This is true of both regular and irregular verbs.

SOME REGULAR VERB FORMS			
PRESENT	**PRESENT PARTICIPLE***	**PAST**	**PAST PARTICIPLE****
care, cares	am caring	cared	have cared
yell, yells	are yelling	yelled	have yelled

SOME IRREGULAR VERB FORMS			
PRESENT	**PRESENT PARTICIPLE***	**PAST**	**PAST PARTICIPLE****
think, thinks	was thinking	thought	has thought
grow, grows	were growing	grew	have grown

IRREGULAR VERBS WHOSE FORM DOES NOT CHANGE			
PRESENT	**PRESENT PARTICIPLE***	**PAST**	**PAST PARTICIPLE****
cost, costs	is costing	cost	has cost
put, puts	am putting	put	have put

*uses *am, is, are, was,* or *were* as helping verb
**uses *have, has,* or *had* as helping verb

Verb Tenses

All verb tenses are formed by utilizing one of the four principal parts of the verb. When we combine these parts with different pronouns, we can see all the different forms that a verb can take in a given tense; this is called **verb conjugation**.

CONJUGATING THE IRREGULAR VERBS *BRING* AND *DO*		
	SINGULAR	PLURAL
PRESENT TENSE		
First person	I bring, do	we bring, do
Second person	you bring, do	you bring, do
Third person	he, she, it brings, does	they bring, do
PAST TENSE		
First person	I brought, did	we brought, did
Second person	you brought, did	you brought, did
Third person	he, she, it brought, did	they brought, did
FUTURE TENSE		
First person	I will bring, will do	we will bring, will do
Second person	you will bring, will do	you will bring, will do
Third person	he, she, it will bring, will do	they will bring, will do

We are most familiar with three basic tenses:

Present. The present tense shows present action or action that happens on a regular basis.

Example:
He **writes** articles for a local newspaper.

Past. The past tense indicates that the action has already happened.

Example:
He **wrote** several award-winning articles.

Future. The future tense tells us that the action has not yet happened, but will.

Example:
He **will write** an editorial for *Time* this month.

TIP

Use the present tense to discuss what you have read in a book, poem, or other text, even if it was written in the past.

Practice

Choose the correct verb and identify the tense in the following sentences.

1. I will (bring, brought) chips and dip to the Super Bowl party.

2. Last week Su Lin (spoke, speaking, speak) with us about her experience with the graduate writing program, and answered our questions about the classes.

3. A photographer will (come, has come, went) out to our house tomorrow to take pictures of my mother's prizewinning orchids.

4. Did you (set, setting) the timer to let us know when the chicken is done?

5. Jeremy (learned, learning, learn) that the bus comes at 7:45 sharp every day, so he needs to leave his house by 7:30 at the latest.

In addition to the three basic verb tenses—present, past, and future—a number of other tenses more precisely pinpoint the timing or progress of actions.

Present Progressive. The present progressive tense shows action that is currently in progress. The present progressive is formed by combining the present tense of the verb *be* with the present participle of a verb.

> **Example:**
> Robert and Olivia **are running** the charity auction at the church.

Past Progressive. The past progressive tense indicates that the action happened at some specific time in the past. The past progressive is formed by combining the past tense of the verb *be* with the present participle of a verb.

> **Example:**
> Jennifer **was watching** the lottery drawing on TV last night.

Future Progressive. The future progressive tense denotes that the action is continuous or will occur in the future. The future progressive is formed by combining the future tense of the verb *be* with the present participle of a verb.

> **Example:**
> Wanda **will be traveling** to Provence next winter.

Practice

Choose the correct verb and identify its tense in the following sentences.

6. We were (eating, eaten) dinner last night when the phone rang.

7. According to the itinerary, he will be (arriving, arrive, arrived) in Denver a little after 4:00 P.M.

8. Whitney is (marking, mark, marked) her name on her lunch in the refrigerator this week, after her yogurt went missing last week.

9. Did you know that the company is (stopped, stopping, stop) the use of nonrecycled materials in its packaging?

Present Perfect. The present perfect tense shows that the action was started in the past and continues up to the present time. The present perfect is formed by combining *have* or *has* with the past participle of a verb.

> **Example:**
> People **have used** money as a means of exchange since about 1200 BCE.

Past Perfect. The past perfect tense indicates that the action happened in the past and was completed before some other past action was begun. The past perfect is formed by combining the helping verb *had* with the past participle of a verb.

> **Example:**
> Before that, many **had bartered** for the goods they wanted with shells, livestock, and agriculture.

Future Perfect. The future perfect tense tells us that the action will start and finish in the future. The future perfect is formed by combining the helping verbs *will have*, *would have*, or *will have been* with the past participle of a verb.

> **Example:**
> As of 2015, the U.S. dollar **will have been used** by its citizens as national currency for about 230 years.

TIP

When you write, pick a verb tense and stick with it. Change tenses only if there is a real change in time. Unnecessary shifts in tense can confuse readers.

Practice

Choose the correct verb and identify the tense in the following sentences.

10. By the time the play is over, we will have (be, been, being) at the theater for more than three hours.

11. When I (baking, baked, bake) with my grandmother, I always learn something new.

12. Once I take this final exam, I will (have, has, having) completed my MBA degree.

13. Tanya is (making, made, make) handmade invitations for her wedding.

14. We (paid, pay, paying) an astronomical amount of money to see the Rolling Stones in concert, but we had so much fun that it was worth it.

15. He has (making, made, make) such a good impression in his first few months here that the managers already want to promote him to the next level.

16. In the photo, Janelle (jumps, jumped, jumping) to block the shot as Mary Anne launches the basketball toward the basket.

17. Thanks to the company's online system, I will (track, tracking, tracked) my package from the warehouse to my door.

18. Julio will (negotiating, negotiate, negotiated) with his boss for a raise, due to his strong sales performance in the past year.

19. Rumor has it that the ghost of Old Mr. Weaver has (haunt, haunted, haunting) that house on the corner for more than 50 years.

20. When Sylvia and Tyrone's cat didn't come home for two days, they (paper, papered, papering) the neighborhood with flyers and pictures of Snuffles in the hope that someone would recognize the cat and bring it home.

TIP

A ghastly grammatical error to avoid is interchanging the words *of* and *have* in writing. Consider the term *should've*, as in "I should've gone with the blue, not the green." It is a common misconception that *should of*, not *should have*, is being said, and it is then written that way. Be careful! The terms *could've* and *would've* (wrongly assumed to be *could of* and *would of*) fall into the same trap.

Answers

1. **will bring:** future tense
2. **spoke:** past tense
3. **will come:** future tense
4. **did set:** past tense
5. **learned:** past tense
6. **were eating:** past progressive tense
7. **will be arriving:** future progressive tense
8. **is marking:** present progressive tense
9. **is stopping:** present progressive tense
10. **will have been:** future perfect tense
11. **bake:** present tense
12. **will have completed:** future perfect tense
13. **is making:** present progressive tense
14. **paid:** past tense
15. **has made:** present perfect tense
16. **jumps:** present tense
17. **will track:** future tense
18. **will negotiate:** future tense
19. **has haunted:** present perfect tense
20. **papered:** past tense

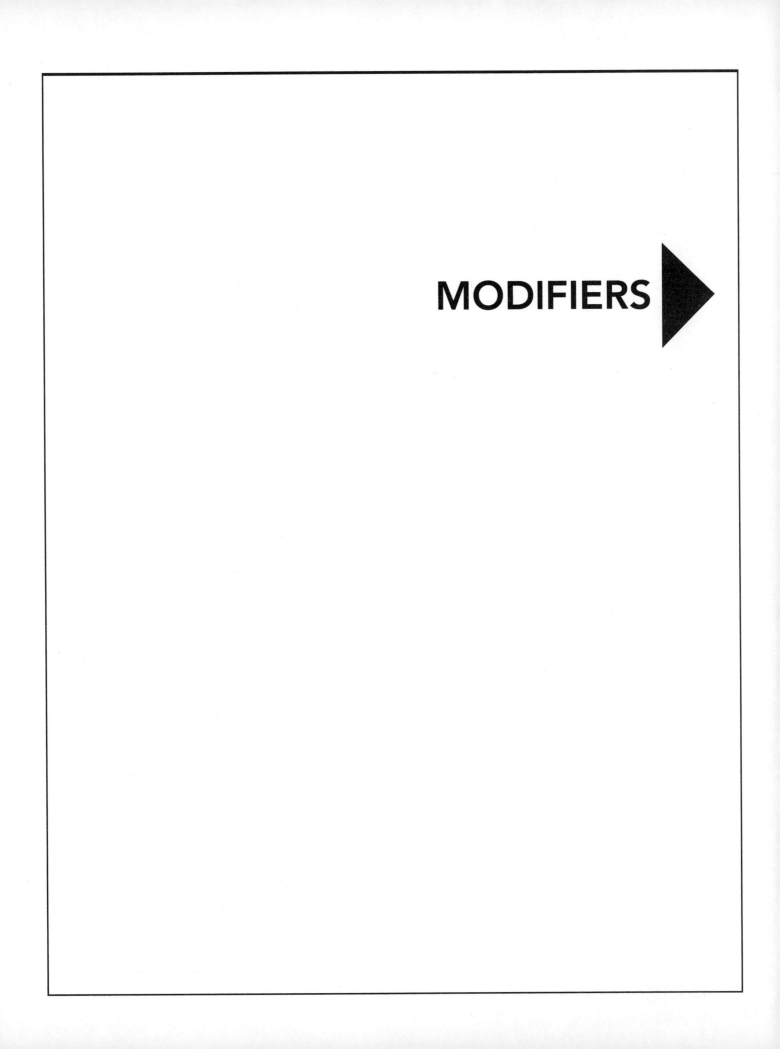

MODIFIERS

7

ADJECTIVES

A man's character may be learned from the adjectives which he habitually uses in conversation.

—Mark Twain, American author and humorist (1835–1910)

LESSON SUMMARY

There's more to this modifier than describing. Learn to identify articles, demonstratives, possessives, and comparatives as well.

Adjectives give a listener or reader more specific information about a noun or pronoun. For instance, if a group of people were asked to think of the word *car*, each person might have a different mental image. That's because the word *car* by iself is too general. But if the words *red* and *convertible* were added, the visual images would be more similar because the car has been described more specifically. An adjective is what we call a **modifier**; it answers any of three specific questions about the noun(s) or pronoun(s) it is modifying: *what kind?* (*friendly, robust, spiky*), *which one(s)?* (*this, that, these, those*), or *how many?* (*nine, few, many, some*).

While adjectives typically come before the noun(s) they are modifying, they may come afterward, too.

Example:
The roller coaster, **large** and **intimidating**, loomed high above all other rides at the park, tantalizing the most daring of park visitors.

Practice

Identify the common adjectives in the following sentences.

1. Jeremy was disappointed when the inky blue stain wouldn't wash out of his favorite shirt.

2. The dog's muddy pawprints showed an incriminating trail of misbehavior all around the house.

3. The public boycott of the violent new video game had little effect—the best-selling game became more popular than ever.

4. The view of Mt. Rushmore was even more breathtaking than Vivian had imagined.

5. Even after the shelf collapsed, her favorite figurine was miraculously unbroken.

TIP

Remember, adjectives paint pictures for a reader or listener. So use colorful adjectives to describe how something or someone looks (*scarlet*, *tall*), sounds (*noisy*, *melodic*), feels (*humid*, *gloomy*), tastes (*bitter*, *chewy*), or smells (*acrid*, *pungent*).

Articles

Three words we use in our everyday language—*a*, *an*, and *the*—are special adjectives called **articles**. There are two types of articles: the definite article (*the*), which implies something specific (not just any road map but this particular road map) and the indefinite article (*a* or *an*), which is nonspecific (pick a road map; any one will do).

TIP

Sometimes deciding whether to use a or an can be tricky. The best way to decide is to use your ears. The word *igloo*, for instance, begins with an initial vowel sound (short *i*), so it takes the indefinite article *an*. The word *ferocious*, on the other hand, begins with an initial consonant sound (*f*), so it takes the indefinite article *a*. But do not let the beginning letter fool you. For instance, although the word one begins with a vowel, it has an initial consonant sound (*w*), so it takes *a*, not *an*.

Practice

Correctly place the indefinite article *a* or *an* in front of each word.

6. heart

7. one-hit wonder

8. hors d'oeuvre

9. egregious error

10. gnome

11. underachiever

12. wishing well

13. wrapped gift

14. IOU

15. quandary

16. mnemonic device

17. whisper

18. yearly appointment

19. yo-yo

20. horror movie

Proper Adjectives

Proper adjectives look like proper nouns because they are capitalized, but they are modifying nouns, and are therefore adjectives. The phrases *English tea*, *Wilson family*, and *Chinese yo-yo* begin with a proper adjective, each answering the question *what kind?* or *which one?* about the noun it is modifying:

What kind of tea?	English
Which family?	Wilson
What kind of yo-yo?	Chinese

Practice
Determine whether the boldfaced word is a proper noun or a proper adjective in the following sentences.

21. We got to sample various kinds of **Swedish** food at the smorgasbord.

22. Whenever I'm in **Denver**, I try to get tickets for a Colorado Rockies game.

23. Our deluxe hotel room had **French** doors that led out onto a balcony overlooking the beach.

24. Devon looked up to her adventurous aunt, who had visited the **Arctic** region on an expedition several years ago.

25. Gary was in the mood for a reuben sandwich, so he was disappointed to learn that the restaurant had run out of **Swiss** cheese.

Pronouns as Adjectives

A **pronoun** such as *he, she,* or *it* takes the place of a noun. If a noun can play the role of an adjective, so, too, can a pronoun. Some personal pronouns fall into the category of possessive adjectives: *my, your, his, her, its, our, their.* Take care not to confuse possessive adjectives with the possessive pronouns *mine, yours, his, hers, ours, theirs.* (You can review pronouns in Lesson 3.) While possessive pronouns can stand alone, a noun must follow a possessive adjective, which answers *which one?* about that noun.

Examples:
Ronald took **his** *lawn mower* to the repair shop.
Victoria and Charles balanced **their** *checkbook* together.
Sara cleaned **her** *room* until it sparkled.

For comparison, here are a few sentences using possessive pronouns. Notice that here the object does *not* follow the pronoun.

That *lawn mower* is **his**.
Those *checkbooks* are **theirs**.
The clean *room* is **hers**.

Practice
Determine whether the boldfaced word is a possessive adjective or a possessive pronoun in the following sentences.

26. **Her** birthday party is scheduled for Friday the 23rd.

27. Even though he followed the recipe, **his** soufflé did not turn out the way he had expected.

28. They made the mess in the kitchen, so the responsibility for cleaning it up is **theirs**.

29. Trina's decision about where to go to college is **hers**, and hers alone.

30. **Our** favorite show comes on Tuesday nights at 9:00.

31. Pete's golf trophy is **his** most prized possession.

32. **My** attempts to learn how to knit resulted in several strange-looking hats.

33. That book over there on the table—is it **yours**?

34. "Be **mine**," the valentine said.

35. "**Your** homework needs to be finished before you go to bed," Mom announced.

Demonstrative Adjectives

Like possessive adjectives, **demonstrative adjectives** (*this, that, these, those*) answer *which one?* about the object, but they always appear *before* the noun being modified.

>   **Examples:**
>   **That** pool looks so inviting on **this** sweltering day.
>   **This** channel always seems to have so many commercials.
>   **These** flowers are exceptionally beautiful in **that** vase.
>   **Those** shoes are so much more comfortable than **that** pair.

If the word *this, that, these, or those* is not followed by a noun, but is *replacing* a noun in the sentence, it is considered a pronoun.

>   **Examples:**
>   **This** is broken.
>   **That** belongs to Shera.
>   **These** are sharp. Be careful.
>   **Those** smell rotten.

Practice
Determine whether the boldfaced word is a demonstrative adjective or a demonstrative pronoun in the following sentences.

36. **That** is the coolest thing I have ever seen.

37. I've never been to **this** part of the city before.

38. Are **these** the kind of flowers Jenny wanted?

39. **These** spicy peppers are much hotter than the kind we usually buy.

40. **That** idea is good, but you should give it some more thought.

41. She picked **that** café on the corner as a meeting place.

42. Can you identify **that** type of butterfly?

43. **This** color looks better on you than that one.

44. Are you sure **this** is the right address?

45. Do you know how much **these** DVDs cost?

Comparative Adjectives

In the course of writing and speaking, it is often necessary to show how one thing compares to another. We can do this with three different levels of adjectives: the positive degree, the comparative degree, and the superlative degree.

In the positive degree, a simple statement is made about the noun:

>   This sushi is **good**.

In the comparative degree, a contrast is made between two nouns:

This sushi is good, but that one is **better**.

In the superlative degree, a comparison is made among more than two nouns:

Of all the sushi, this is the **best**.

Here are some rules to remember in forming the comparative or the superlative degree:

Rule 1. Add -er and -est to most one-syllable adjectives, like *small, smaller, smallest*; *hot, hotter, hottest*. Some one-syllable adjectives are irregular, like *good* (*good, better, best*), *bad* (*bad, worse, worst*), and *many* (*many, more, most*).

Rule 2. For adjectives of two or more syllables, use *more* and *most* to enhance the degree, or *less* and *least* to decrease the degree.

Examples:
agreeable: *more* agreeable, *most* agreeable; *less* agreeable, *least* agreeable
spotted: *more* spotted, *most* spotted; *less* spotted, *least* spotted

Of course, there are always exceptions. Here are some two-syllable adjectives that allow you to use -ier and -iest in the comparative degree and the superlative degree. Note that the final -y is changed to an -i before the endings are added.

happy, happier, happiest
picky, pickier, pickiest
silly, sillier, silliest

Lastly, some adjectives just cannot be compared no matter how hard you try; they are called absolute adjectives or incomparables. Consider, for instance, the word *unique*: How can anything that is already one-of-a-kind be *more unique*? Other absolute adjectives are *favorite, true, false, perfect, round, square, free,* and *complete*.

TIP
A simple tip: Add *more* or *most* before a long adjective—*more frightened, more harmonious, most ridiculous, most delectable*.

Practice
Determine which form of the adjective best completes each of the following sentences.

46. Micah's (best, better, good) subject is creative writing.

47. His book sales were slightly (highest, higher) than his rival's.

48. The doctor told me that my cholesterol needs to be (lower, low, lowest) than it is now.

49. After six years of art classes, she is (adepter, more adept) at drawing than I am.

50. Dad stayed home sick because he felt (worst, worser, worse) this morning than he did yesterday.

Answers

1. inky, blue, favorite
2. muddy, incriminating
3. public, violent, new, best-selling, popular
4. breathtaking
5. favorite, unbroken
6. a heart
7. a one-hit wonder
8. an hors d'oeuvre
9. an egregious error
10. a gnome
11. an underachiever
12. a wishing well
13. a wrapped gift
14. an IOU
15. a quandary
16. a mnemonic device
17. a whisper
18. a yearly appointment
19. a yo-yo
20. a horror movie
21. proper adjective
22. proper noun
23. proper adjective
24. proper adjective

25. proper adjective
26. possessive adjective
27. possessive adjective
28. possessive pronoun
29. possessive pronoun
30. possessive adjective
31. possessive adjective
32. possessive adjective
33. possessive pronoun
34. possessive pronoun
35. possessive adjective
36. demonstrative pronoun
37. demonstrative adjective
38. demonstrative pronoun
39. demonstrative adjective
40. demonstrative adjective
41. demonstrative adjective
42. demonstrative adjective
43. demonstrative adjective
44. demonstrative pronoun
45. demonstrative adjective
46. best
47. higher
48. lower
49. more adept
50. worse

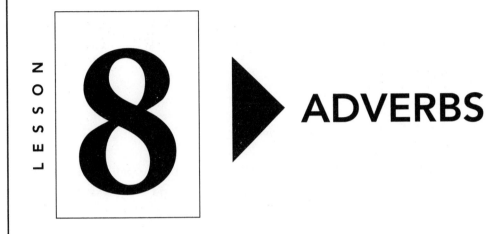

8 ▶ ADVERBS

I'm glad you like adverbs. I adore them; they are the only qualifications I really much respect.

—Henry James, American-born English
author and critic (1843–1916)

LESSON SUMMARY
Degrees of comparison can be tricky, as can distinguishing between adjectives and adverbs. Learn which is which, and why.

Adverbs are also called modifiers. Whereas adjectives modify nouns, adverbs most frequently modify verbs. Adverbs can also modify adjectives and even other adverbs.

An adverb answers four specific questions about the word it modifies: *where?* (*here, inside, there, across, out*), *when?* (*never, tomorrow, afterward, before, while*), *how?* (*irritatingly, swiftly, suspiciously, fervently*), and *to what extent?* (*so, very, too, extremely, really*).

Memorizing these questions will help you identify adverbs. You can also look for words that end in *-ly*, as long as you remember that not all such words are adverbs. For example, *friendly, neighborly, costly, ugly, burly, lovely,* and *cowardly* are adjectives, not adverbs.

The table that follows shows examples of how adverbs are used. For clarification, the adverbs are boldfaced, and the words they modify are underlined.

ADVERBS MODIFY . . .		
Verbs	Some trains **always** <u>run</u> on time.	Margaret <u>answered</u> **quickly**.
Adjectives	. . . a **really** <u>tough</u> professor	. . . a **rather** <u>suspicious</u> character.
Other Adverbs	. . . spoke **so** <u>eloquently</u>	. . . argues **very** <u>effectively</u>

Practice

Identify the common adverbs in the following sentences.

1. We are extremely lucky that the rain held off until after the graduation ceremony.

2. You and I should take a cross-country road trip sometime.

3. The test was really difficult, but I knew I had truly done my best.

4. She sent daily reminders because she knew she would forget to water her woefully neglected plants.

5. Taking Miller Street is the way to get there quickly.

Comparative Adverbs

Just as adjectives can show degrees of comparison, so can adverbs, with the words *more*, *most*, *less*, and *least*, and the suffixes *-er* and *-est*. A comparative adverb contrasts two words; a superlative compares three or more. Follow these rules for making adverbs for comparing:

Rule 1. One-syllable adverbs use the *-er* and *-est* endings.

Example:
fast—faster—fastest

Rule 2. Two-syllable adverbs use *more* and *most* to enhance the degree, or *less* and *least* to decrease the degree.

Examples:
quickly—more quickly—most quickly
often—less often—least often

Rule 3. Irregular adverbs do not follow either form.

Examples:
well—better—best
much—more—most

TIP

Absolute adverbs—words like *all*, *every*, *completely*, and *entirely*—already refer to everything possible, and therefore cannot be intensified any further. Similarly, *never* and *always*, two extremes of *when*, would be difficult to use in the comparative and superlative.

Practice

Determine which form of the adverb best completes each of the following sentences.

6. Breaking my leg was the (worse, worst, worser) pain I have ever experienced.

7. Everyone was sad to see Grandpa go home after his visit, but I think I was the (distraughtest, most distraught) of all of us.

8. Shelly bought that car because it was deemed the (safer, safe, safest) out of the ten brands in the recent survey.

9. We go to Joe's Burger World (oftener, most often, more often) than we go to Andy's House of Pizzas.

10. Due to delays on the subway, several people got to the meeting late, but I got there the (latest, later, most late) of everyone.

Distinguishing between Adverbs and Adjectives

It is not unusual to encounter words that look like they are one part of speech when, in fact, they are playing the role of another.

Examples:
The bird arrived **early** and caught the worm.
The **early** bird catches the worm.

In the first sentence, *early* is an adverb modifying the verb *arrived*, answering the question *when did the bird arrive?—early*. In the second sentence, *early* is an adjective modifying the noun *bird*, answering the question *what kind of bird is it?—an early* bird.

The following table gives some examples of adverbs and adjectives that share the same form. The adverbs and adjectives are boldfaced, and the words being modified are underlined.

Some adjectives and adverbs can be a bit troublesome because they appear interchangeable but are not.

ADVERBS AND ADJECTIVES THAT SHARE THE SAME FORM	
ADJECTIVE	ADVERB
His bike is **fast**.	He pedals **fast**.
The paper contained only a **straight** line.	You must go **straight** home.
Close friends are a treasure.	Brian and Theresa sat **close** together.
Marcia keeps her **daily** routine simple.	Exercising **daily** is good for your heart.
Other words that fall into this category are *high, late, far, hard, long, low, right, wrong,* and *wide.*	

Good and Well

The word *good* is *always* an adjective, never an adverb. *Good* implies *satisfactory* or *commendable*.

> **Examples:**
> You did a **good** job as PR rep.
> John is such a **good** map reader.

Well can be an adjective *or* an adverb. As an adverb, it implies *how something is done*.

> **Examples:**
> The team played **well** this season.
> Katelyn can swim freestyle **well**.

As an adjective, *well* is used with a linking verb and usually refers to someone's health.

> **Examples:**
> Julia looked **well** enough to go back to school this morning.
> Our cat seems **well** after the successful surgery.

Bad and Badly

Bad is always an adjective, so it can only modify a noun or a pronoun after a linking verb.

> **Examples:**
> That cough of yours sounds pretty **bad**.
> The cream seems **bad**, so throw it out.

Badly, on the other hand, is an adverb and can only modify an action verb. It tells *how something is done*.

> **Examples:**
> The clown performs magic **badly**.
> My little brother behaved **badly** at dinner.

Most and Almost

Most can be an adjective when it refers to an amount of something.

> **Examples:**
> **Most** cars run solely on gasoline.
> It seems that **most** owners agreed.

Or it can be an adverb used to form the superlative degree of an adjective in a sentence.

> **Examples:**
> They were the **most** surprised.
> This is the **most** intelligent dog I've ever seen.

Almost, on the other hand, is an adverb that modifies the adjectives *every* and *all* and the adverbs *always* and *never* in a sentence. *Almost* can also be placed before a main verb as an indication of degree.

> **Examples:**
>
> | | |
> |---|---|
> | Adjectives | Amy has **almost every** album the Beatles ever recorded. |
> | | Christian ate **almost all** the ice cream in one sitting. |
> | Adverbs | They **almost always** participate in the annual softball game. |
> | | He **almost never** leaves without saying good-bye. |
> | Verbs | She is **almost** finished with her painting. |

TIP

The word *not* is an adverb that makes a sentence negative. Place the *not* before an action verb. (*He could not paint.*) Place the *not* after a form of *be*. (*We are not lost.*)

Practice

Determine whether the boldfaced words in the following sentences are adjectives or adverbs.

11. My impatience grew as I spent more time on the **slow** line.

12. You should drive more **slowly**, unless you want to get a speeding ticket.

13. That was the **most** fun I remember having at one of these events.

14. **Most** people in my neighborhood have lived here for at least five years.

15. He **almost** never shows up to the weekly meetings, so we were quite surprised to see him sitting there waiting for the rest of us as we came in.

16. They have **almost** every issue of "Spiderman" ever produced.

17. That movie was so **bad**, we didn't even want to stay for the end of it.

18. The magician performed so **badly** that it ended up seeming more like a comedy show instead.

19. The peanut butter cookies were so **good**, I went back for more.

20. I was surprised by how **well** the team did this year, considering they won no games last year.

Answers

1. extremely
2. sometime
3. really, truly
4. woefully
5. quickly
6. worst
7. most distraught
8. safest
9. more often
10. latest
11. adjective
12. adverb
13. adjective
14. adjective
15. adverb
16. adverb
17. adjective
18. adverb
19. adjective
20. adverb

TIP

When you use adverbs correctly, they enhance your writing. But too many can become annoying. Use them only when they are really needed.

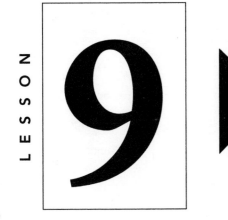

▶ PREPOSITIONS

From now on, ending a sentence with a preposition is something up with which I will not put.

—Winston Churchill, British author
and prime minister (1874–1965)

LESSON SUMMARY
What's an OOP and where are they found? Find out in this lesson.

Like an adverb, a **preposition** conveys a relationship, usually of time (*when*) or place (*where*), between certain words in a sentence. A **prepositional phrase** is a small group of words that begins with a preposition and ends with a noun or pronoun. The noun or pronoun at the end of the phrase is called the **object of the preposition (OOP)**.

Examples:
across town
beyond the realm **of** understanding
under the guise **of** reality
upon your approval
according to the polls

COMMON PREPOSITIONS					
about	above	across	after	against	along
among	around	as	at	before	behind
below	beneath	beside	between	beyond	but
by	concerning	despite	down	during	except
for	from	in	into	like	near
next	of	off	on	onto	out
outside	over	past	since	through	throughout
to	toward	under	underneath	unlike	until
up	upon	with	within	without	

The following compound prepositions are also common:

prior to	next to	on top of	because of	in addition to
in place of	according to	in front of	on account of	aside from

Practice

Identify the prepositional phrases in the following sentences.

1. At this restaurant, the waiters sing to you on your birthday.

2. Getting to the Olympics has been his goal ever since he was a little kid swimming around the shallow end of the pool.

3. The store you're looking for is around the corner, on Bleecker Street.

4. I finally found my glasses under the papers on my desk, after searching all over the house.

5. "You hit it right on the nose," she said when I guessed the answer.

Distinguishing between Prepositions and Adverbs

How can you tell if a word is a preposition and not an adverb? If the word begins a prepositional phrase, then it is a preposition. If it does not, it is an adverb. In the following sentence, *before* is an adverb because it does not begin a phrase; it stands by itself and is not followed by a noun.

I have never seen that person **before**.

But in the following sentence, *before* is a preposition because it is followed by a noun, creating a prepositional phrase.

She stood **before** the judge to make her plea.

TIP

Although a prepositional phrase contains a noun or pronoun, that noun or pronoun can never be the subject of the sentence. Prove it: Circle the prepositional phrase in the previous sentence. A noun or pronoun that is left outside the circle is your subject.

Sometimes you may come across sentences that end with prepositions. Some are grammatically correct, but others are not. You can figure out whether the sentence is correct by rewording it using the same words. If it makes sense, it is fine. But if it does not, it is grammatically incorrect.

Example:

Crime is something I worry about.

Reworded:

Something I worry about is crime. (Grammatically correct)

Example:

It is a problem I need help with.

Reworded:

A problem I need help with is it. (Grammatically incorrect)

Remedy:

It is a problem with which I need help.

Sometimes it is awkward to reword a sentence that ends with a preposition.

Example:

Indicate which person you are talking about.

Becomes:

Indicate about which person you are talking.

Example:

She brought her brushes to paint with.

Becomes:

She brought her brushes with which to paint.

You may have heard or been taught that a sentence should never end in a preposition. But in modern English, this rule has been relaxed to avoid awkward constructions. Now, the tendency is to use your discretion in such a situation and go with what feels right.

Practice

Determine whether the boldfaced word is a preposition or an adverb.

6. Our team lost, but we were cheered **up** when we stopped to get ice cream **after**.

7. Everyone at the table **except** Mary ordered the steak.

8. **Throughout** the day, it's important to drink plenty **of** water.

9. If you don't hurry up, you'll fall **behind**.

10. **According to** Raj, we should be there in **about** 20 minutes.

11. I get motion sickness on those rides where you spin **around** and **around**.

12. We talked about this **before**: It's your responsibility to walk the dog **in** the morning.

13. Mrs. Phillips took me **aside** and asked if I would mind giving a quick talk introducing the keynote speaker.

14. All of the gift-wrapping was done **by** Jeff and Marnie.

15. When she couldn't find her grandmother's antique watch, she was **beside** herself **with** worry that it wouldn't turn **up**.

Prepositional phrases may end with double nouns or pronouns, forming compound OOPs. (*I went to England and France with her and him.*)

Answers

1. at this restaurant; on your birthday
2. to the Olympics; around the shallow end; of the pool
3. around the corner; on Bleecker Street
4. under the papers; on my desk; over the house
5. on the nose
6. adverb; adverb
7. preposition
8. preposition; preposition
9. adverb
10. preposition; adverb
11. adverb; adverb
12. adverb; preposition
13. adverb
14. preposition
15. preposition; preposition; adverb

10 ▶ MISPLACED MODIFIERS AND TRICKY WORDS

Words differently arranged have a different meaning, and meanings differently arranged have different effects.

—Blaise Pascal, French scientist
and philosopher (1623–1662)

LESSON SUMMARY

Learn to manage those bothersome squinting, split, dangling, and disruptive modifiers that rear their heads when you least expect it.

Misplaced Modifiers

When you write, you transfer what you are thinking—what you want to say—onto paper for someone else to read. You use modifiers to describe words or make their meanings more specific. You know what you mean to say, but your message can become unclear if you have misplaced modifiers: phrases or clauses that slip into the wrong place in your sentences.

There is a simple way to prevent your modifiers from becoming misplaced: Keep them as close as possible to the words they modify.

Dangling Modifiers

A **dangling modifier** does just that: It dangles and doesn't seem to modify any word in particular.

Examples:

After burning dinner, Russell opened the door in his pajamas to let the smoke out.

After burning dinner in his pajamas, Russell opened the door to let the smoke out.

Both sentences make it sound as though Russell cooked dinner inside his pajamas, burned the dinner, and opened the door to air out his pajamas.

This error is easily corrected by placing the prepositional phrase *in his pajamas* closer to the word it is modifying (*Russell*), and placing the adverb phrase *after burning dinner* later in the sentence.

Corrected:

In his pajamas, Russell opened the door after burning dinner to let the smoke out.

Russell, in his pajamas, opened the door to let the smoke out after he burned dinner.

Squinting Modifiers

A **squinting modifier** is one that's ambiguous because of its placement—it seems to describe something on either side of it.

Example:

Ryan's teacher, Ms. Bennett, told him when he completed his test to pass out some papers for her.

Did Ms. Bennett tell Ryan she wanted him to complete his test before passing out some papers for her? Or had Ryan already finished his test when Ms. Bennett told him to help her pass out papers?

Corrected:

When he completed his test, Ryan's teacher, Ms. Bennett, asked him to pass out some papers.

Ryan's teacher, Ms. Bennett, told him he could pass out some papers once he had completed his test.

Split Infinitives

Infinitives are *to* verbs, and modifiers do not belong between the two words.

Incorrect: My mom told me **to** never **lie**.
Corrected: My mom told me never **to lie**.

Disruptive Modifiers

When a modifying clause is improperly placed within a sentence, it disrupts the flow of the words.

Example:

I will not tolerate, just because you're the star, your disrespectful outbursts.

Corrected:

I will not tolerate your disrespectful outbursts just because you're the star.

Managing Your Modifiers

Here are a few rules to help you place modifiers correctly in a sentence.

Rule 1. Place simple adjectives before the nouns they modify.

Example:

Wearing a **green** raincoat, the exhausted student walked home in the rain.

Rule 2. Place adjective phrases and adjective clauses after the nouns being modified.

Example:
The surfer **with long blond hair** rode the ten-foot wave with ease.

Rule 3. Place *only*, *barely*, *just*, and *almost* before the noun or verb being modified. Their placement determines the message in your sentence.

Examples:
Only Peter ran to the store. [No one else but Peter went.]
Peter **only** ran to the store. [He didn't walk.]
Peter ran **only** to the store. [He didn't go anywhere else.]
Peter ran to the **only** store. [There was no other store around but that one.]
Peter ran to the store **only**. [He ran to the store, and did nothing else.]

TIP

The most frequently misplaced modifier is the word *only*. It shows limit or contrast and, as previously shown, placing *only* next to the word it modifies will really clarify what you are trying to say.

Practice
Rewrite each sentence so that the modifiers are properly placed.

1. Dripping constantly, I tightened the leaky faucet.

2. I was taught to always treat people the way I want to be treated.

3. Cooking dinner, the cat ran under my feet and almost made me drop the pot roast.

4. Green and soft, I was proud of the scarf I'd knitted myself.

5. We're all packed, and ready to happily go on vacation.

Tricky Words

As you've noticed, words in the English language can be tricky. Homonyms, homophones, and homographs remind us that not only should we know how to spell words, but we should also know what each word means and which spelling of a word to use!

Homonyms
Homonyms are words that are spelled and pronounced the same but have different meanings. They are often called "multiple-meaning words."

HOMONYMS	
pine	I **pine** for the **pine** trees of my native Black Forest.
well	Stacy didn't feel **well** after drinking the water from the **well**.

Homophones
Homophones are words that sound the same but are spelled differently and have different meanings. The following chart lists some familiar sound-alike homophones.

	HOMOPHONES
ad/add	I clipped the **ad** in the newspaper. **Add** the items up to get the total.
aisle/isle/I'll	The grocery **aisle** was messy and chaotic. They bought a small **isle** in the Gulf of Mexico. **I'll** show you how to do this.
allowed/aloud	No one is **allowed** in my office without permission. I heard him read my name **aloud** today.
ant/aunt	I saw an **ant** carry a crumb up the table leg. **Aunt** Myrtle is eccentric.
ate/eight	Dad **ate** a rack of ribs at dinner. There are **eight** people in my family.
bare/bear	Old Mother Hubbard's cupboard was **bare**. **Bear** hunting is illegal in some states.
blew/blue	Linda **blew** her birthday candles out. One **blue** sock was missing.
brake/break	Tap the **brake** gently when stopping in snow. Give me a **break**, please.
buy/by	Can you **buy** milk on your way home? They quickly ran **by** the store.
cent/scent/sent	One **cent** is called a penny. I recognized the **scent** of her perfume immediately. Greg **sent** flowers to Dahlia on Mother's Day.
chews/choose	My dog **chews** on almost anything. May I **choose** the next game to play?
colonel/kernel	Grandpa Jim was a **colonel** in the Army. Don't bite on the popcorn **kernel**.
dear/deer	She is such a **dear** friend. **Deer** roam the woods beside my house.
dew/do/due	The morning **dew** felt cold on my feet. I **do** not like licorice. The first payment is **due** in four days.
ewe/yew/you	The **ewe** watched her lamb closely. A small evergreen called a **yew** is prevalent on most continents. I love **you**.

HOMOPHONES *(continued)*

flew/flu/flue	They **flew** to Orlando for the first time. It is not easy to catch the **flu**. The chimney **flue** was dirty.
flour/flower	**Flour** is used to make many desserts. The **flower** lasted only four days in the vase.
heal/heel/he'll	Wounds **heal** at different rates. Her **heel** hurt after she took her new shoe off. **He'll** be the best choice, I think.
hear/here	Can you **hear** well? **Here** are the apples from the basket.
hole/whole	The **hole** they dug was three feet deep. I can't believe I ate the **whole** sandwich.
hour/our	Within the next **hour**, you will see a real difference. **Our** friends are moving in September.
knew/new	He **knew** better than to do that. Our **new** neighbors built a deck.
knot/not	I tried to untie the **knot** in her shoestring. They could **not** see because of the fog.
know/no	I **know** how to jog backward. **No**, he doesn't.
meat/meet	The **meat** at her butcher shop is fresh. Let's **meet** next week to finish this.
need/kneed/knead	I **need** a vacation; do you? Nathan got **kneed** in the side by his opponent. You must **knead** the bread dough before letting it rise.
one/won	Eileen has **one** more hour of work left. Ashley wished she had **won** the prize.
pair/pear	Hillary's **pair** of shoes was two sizes too small. Baked **pear** is easy to make.
peak/peek/pique	We stood at the **peak** of the mountain in awe. He took a quick **peek** in her shopping bag. What I overheard began to **pique** my curiosity.
principal/principle	The **principal** idea is to help others. It's the **principle** of the matter, and nothing else.

HOMOPHONES (continued)

rain/reign/rein   Will it **rain** again tomorrow?
King Henry VIII's **reign** over England lasted 38 years.
The horse's **rein** was worn and needed replacing.

right/rite/write   Turn **right** at the light up ahead.
The tribe's **rite** of passage involved marriage.
Teachers often ask students to **write** essays.

sail/sale   Jan will **sail** in the Caribbean for one week.
I bought the living room furniture on **sale**.

scene/seen   **Scene** four in the play was the turning point in the plot.
I have never **seen** an octopus before.

stationary/stationery   The guard stood **stationary** for several hours.
The pink **stationery** had her monogram on it.

there/their/they're   **There** is a chance that we can go.
It took **their** bus 18 hours to get home.
They're supposed to confirm the appointment.

threw/through   The child **threw** a tantrum in the middle of the store.
Through thick and thin, the friends remained loyal.

to/too/two   I will try **to** change this lightbulb with one hand.
He plays video games **too** often.
My **two** sisters look alike.

which/witch   **Which** sneaker you choose is solely up to you.
Dorothy outsmarted the wicked **witch** in her own castle.

who's/whose   **Who's** going to Albany with Craig tomorrow?
Is this **whose** coat you thought it would be?

wood/would   Pile the **wood** by the back of the shed.
Would you care to give me a hand?

Homographs

Homographs are words that are spelled the same but are pronounced differently and have completely different meanings. Following are some familiar examples.

HOMOGRAPHS	
address	You should **address** the envelope with the **address** on the label.
bass	He is a **bass** fisherman, and also plays the **bass** in a rock band.
bow	I was asked to **bow** to the king and remove my **bow** and arrows.
close	My manager will **close** up tonight; luckily he lives **close** by.
conflict	The reports **conflict** about the recent **conflict** in Congress.
desert	The soldier did not **desert** his unit stationed in the **desert**.
does	He **does** see the **does** standing off to the side of the road.
dove	The **dove dove** toward the flock of gulls to defend his mate.
house	The **house** around the corner will **house** your dog while you're away.
lead	He had finally taken the **lead** in the crossword competition when the **lead** of his pencil broke.
live	I **live** next to the arena, so I'll see many **live** concerts.
minute	The **minute** I saw her, she hounded me about the most **minute** details on the contract.
number	The greater **number** of snow cones I ate, the **number** my tongue became.
present	It was an honor to **present** this special **present** to the winner.
produce	Many farms **produce produce** during the summer.
read	I will **read** the same book you **read** last summer.
record	Don't forget to **record** his high-jump **record** in the books.
resume	Let's **resume** updating your **resume** tomorrow.
separate	**Separate** your socks by color and place them in a **separate** drawer in your dresser.
tear	"Don't **tear** my book!" the little girl said with a **tear** in her eye.
use	I don't have any **use** for this, so feel free to **use** it!
wind	With the **wind** so strong, I couldn't **wind** the string of the kite easily.
wound	He **wound** up wrapping his **wound** with gauze.

Practice

Read each set of clues and figure out which words fit the descriptions. Then indicate if the word pairs are homonyms, homophones, or homographs.

6. precipitation/a monarch's era

7. sturdy building material/past tense of *will*

8. to write something down/the best time in a race

9. the front of a ship/to bend at the waist as a sign of respect

10. two of a kind/oddly shaped fruit

11. type of something/nice to others

12. one one-hundredth of a dollar/an aroma

13. plunged/white bird that symbolizes peace

14. section of a grocery store/land mass in a body of water

15. fruits and vegetables/to create something

16. to pick up where you left off/a document you submit for a job

17. to abandon/a bowl of ice cream

18. three feet/section of land around a house

19. naked/large, furry mammal

20. to move below the surface/part of a kitchen

21. military rank/raw piece of corn

22. tool that creates fire/two items that are alike

23. tiny/one-sixtieth of an hour

24. to speak to/where you live

25. writing paper/unmoving

Answers

Answers for questions 1–5 are suggestions. Your answers may vary.

1. I tightened the leaky faucet, which was dripping constantly.
2. I was taught always to treat people the way I want to be treated.
3. While I was cooking dinner, the cat ran under my feet and almost made me drop the pot roast.
4. I was proud of the green, soft scarf I'd knitted myself.
5. We're all packed, and happily ready to go on vacation.
6. rain/reign: homophones
7. wood/would: homophones
8. record/record: homographs
9. bow/bow: homonyms
10. pair/pear: homophones
11. kind/kind: homonyms
12. cent/scent: homophones
13. dove/dove: homographs
14. aisle/isle: homophones
15. produce/produce: homographs
16. resume/resume: homographs
17. desert/dessert: homophones
18. yard/yard: homonyms
19. bare/bear: homophones
20. sink/sink: homonyms
21. colonel/kernel: homophones
22. match/match: homonyms
23. minute/minute: homographs
24. address/address: homographs
25. stationery/stationary: homophones

SENTENCE STRUCTURE

11 ▶ SENTENCE BASICS

Certain brief sentences are peerless in their ability to give one the feeling that nothing remains to be said.

—Jean Rostand, French historian and biologist (1894–1977)

LESSON SUMMARY

To be a sentence, a group of words must express a complete idea and include a subject and a verb. Basic sentence structure may sound simple, but it goes far beyond just subjects and verbs. In this lesson, learn what complements are and how they come into play when putting together a good sentence.

The fundamental component of speech and writing, sentences help people communicate their ideas to others. Every complete sentence is made up of two major components: a **subject**—a noun or pronoun that tells *whom* or *what* the sentence is about—and a **predicate**—a verb that tells what the subject is *doing* or what *condition* the subject is in.

Subjects

Finding the subject of a sentence is as simple as asking *who?* or *what?* in relation to the verb. In the following examples, the subject is underlined once and the verb is underlined twice.

A subject can be a proper noun:

S   V

Thomas updates his resume regularly.

Who updates? **Thomas**; thus, Thomas is the subject.

A subject can be a common noun:

S   V

The real estate market fluctuates yearly.

What fluctuates? The **market**; thus, market is the subject.

A subject can be a pronoun:

S   V

They traveled overseas for the meeting.

Who traveled? **They**; thus, They is the subject.

A subject can be compound (two or more nouns playing an equal role in the sentence):

S   S   V

Books and the Internet contain helpful information.

What contain? **Books** and the **Internet**; thus, Books and Internet play an equal role in the compound subject.

Although the subject is typically found at the beginning of the sentence, it can also appear elsewhere.

In the middle:

S   V

Before lunch, Michelle decided to run quickly to the bank.

At the end:

V   S

At the end of the pier sat the lone fisherman.

Tricky Subjects

Not all sentences have an obvious, or stated, noun or pronoun as a subject; sometimes the subject is implied. Imperative sentences (sentences that make a request or a command) always have an implied subject:

Wash your hands frequently during the day to prevent colds.

If you ask yourself **who** or **what** wash? there is not a noun in the sentence that answers the question. That is because the subject is *implied*; it is the pronoun **you:**

S   V

(You) wash your hands frequently during the day to prevent colds.

To find the subject in a question, turn it into a statement that places the subject before the verb:

Did Ed go to the convention in Seattle?

becomes:

S   V

Ed went to the convention in Seattle.

You can then ask yourself **Who** went? **Ed** is your subject.

Practice

Identify the simple subject in the following sentences.

1. Overcome by the heat, Mr. Sanchez decided to stay inside for the afternoon.

2. The pharmacist's assistant handed me my prescription.

3. The secret ingredient in my grandmother's famous spaghetti sauce is crushed red pepper flakes.

4. She and I argued constantly when we were kids.

5. Please take your shoes off before coming inside.

6. Can Susie come with us to the movies?

7. A few minutes after 11, Gus finally showed up.

8. The hamsters' cage needs to be cleaned.

9. The presidential motorcade shut down several blocks in New York City for more than an hour.

10. Can't make it to the meeting on Wednesday? Come to the make-up session on Saturday morning.

Predicates

Predicates tell something about the subject or subjects in a sentence. The verb, known as the **simple predicate**, expresses the action done by or to the subject or tells about its condition. You can find the simple predicate in a sentence by asking yourself which word indicates action being done by or to the subject or conveys the condition of the subject.

Examples:

S   V
She approached her supervisor about her recent performance review.

S
The itinerary for Joseph's business trip
V
was changed.

S   V
Meghan was energetic and results-driven.

Like subjects, predicates can be single or compound, which means there are two or more verbs relating to the same subject or compound subject in the sentence.

Examples:

S   V   V   V
At practice, we stretch, run, drill, and
V
scrimmage.

S   S   V
Last Monday, George and Marty arrived late and
V
ran two extra laps.

Practice

Identify the simple predicate in the following sentences.

11. After a lecture about waiting until the last minute on homework, my dad helped me with my project the night before the science fair.

12. Their return flight was canceled due to the stormy weather.

13. Andrew Jackson became the nation's seventh president in 1829.

14. The kids were thrilled to see Aunt Mary, three days earlier than expected.

15. The hunt commenced with the blaring horns and barking dogs.

16. My favorite fruits are oranges, mangoes, and strawberries.

17. Would you please pass the gravy?

18. The handshake sealed the deal.

19. Ideally, my agent will book me another acting job soon.

20. Mark marked the calendar with a red marker.

Complements

The purpose of good communication is to get your message across clearly. Sometimes a sentence has a clear message with just a subject and a verb:

> Stanley left.
> Please reply.
> What gives?
> Did you go?

Other sentences may require more information to complete their meaning:

> Kyle picked _____.
> Gina took _____.

The additional parts that these sentences require are called **complements**.

Examples:
Kyle picked Andrew first.
Gina took a breath.

The complements *Andrew* and *breath* complete the meaning in these sentences by telling us *what* the subjects *picked* and *took*. Complements can include direct objects, indirect objects, predicate nouns, and predicate adjectives.

Direct and Indirect Objects

A **direct object** is a complement in a sentence with an *action verb*. It is a noun or pronoun that "directly" relates to the action verb and receives action from that verb. Direct objects answer **whom?** or **what?** about the action verb.

Examples:

S V D.O.
Kyle picked Andrew first.   Picked whom? *Andrew.*

S V D.O.
Gina took a breath.   Took what? a *breath*

Like subjects and predicates, direct objects can also be **compound**: One or more verbs share more than one object.

Example:

S V
Wanda, a successful real estate agent, listed and

V D.O. D.O.
sold a house and a farm this week.

> ### TIP
> Every sentence must have a subject, but not every sentence will have an object.

A sentence that has a direct object can also have an **indirect object**. It tells which person or thing is the recipient of the direct object, so you cannot have an indirect object without a direct object. You can easily identify an indirect object by asking yourself *to or for whom?* or *to or for what?* after an action verb. Indirect objects are usually placed between the verb and the direct object.

Example:

S V I.O.
The car salesperson showed Chris the latest
D.O.
Mustang GT model.

Practice

Identify the direct and indirect object (if any) in the following sentences.

21. I taught Melissa the song.

22. Mr. Matthews showed me how to do the algebra problems.

23. The cook made Jim a perfect omelet.

24. The photographer managed to get the picture with all of us in it.

25. Jack gave me a piece of advice to help with my problem.

26. I bought overripe bananas for a banana bread recipe.

27. Mickey gave me a musical birthday card that played the theme from my favorite TV show.

28. The environmental group hands people their rally flyers on that corner.

29. I got that bruise while playing soccer.

30. George found my glasses and handed them back to me.

Predicate Nouns and Predicate Adjectives

Known as **subject complements**, predicate nouns rename the subject, and predicate adjectives describe the subject. They are used in sentences with linking verbs, not action verbs.

When a predicate noun follows a linking verb, the linking verb acts like an equals sign (=):

$$\underset{\text{S}}{\underline{\text{DeVaughn}}}\ \underset{\text{V}}{\underline{\text{is}}}\ \text{the}\ \boxed{\underset{\text{P.N.}}{\text{coach}}}.\qquad \textbf{means}$$
DeVaughn = the coach.

Predicate nouns can also be compound in form, so long as they are identifying the same noun:

$$\underset{\text{S}}{\underline{\text{Carla}}}\ \underset{\text{V}}{\underline{\text{was}}}\ \boxed{\underset{\text{P.N.}}{\text{professor}}}\ \text{and}\ \boxed{\underset{\text{P.N.}}{\text{mentor}}}\ \text{to many}$$
students.

Predicate adjectives also follow a linking verb, describe or modify the subject, and can be compound in form as well:

$$\text{Following the interview, }\underset{\text{S}}{\underline{\text{Bill}}}\ \underset{\text{V}}{\underline{\text{felt}}}\ \boxed{\underset{\text{P.A.}}{\text{excited}}}\ \text{and}$$
$$\boxed{\underset{\text{P.A.}}{\text{optimistic}}}.$$

Remember that *complement* means "add to or complete." Predicate nouns and predicate adjectives add to or complete an idea to make it more precise or clear.

Practice

Identify the predicate nouns and predicate adjectives in the following sentences.

31. Mim is the proud owner of a pampered calico cat named Sage.

32. The crocodiles became new members of the reptile exhibit.

33. As a young man, Grandfather was a sailor and traveled the world.

34. Dachshunds are short-legged dogs, sometimes referred to as "wiener dogs" because of their sausage-shaped bodies.

35. Canvas hammocks became popular with the English Navy in the 1600s.

36. Parking spaces in any large city can be difficult to find.

37. Slips are docking spaces for boats.

38. Salads are healthy with the right kind of dressing.

39. Janine is a middle school teacher in Muncie, Indiana.

40. Key limes are popular in drinks, desserts, and marinades.

Answers

1. Mr. Sanchez
2. assistant
3. ingredient
4. she and I
5. [you]
6. Susie
7. Gus
8. cage
9. motorcade
10. [you]
11. helped
12. was canceled
13. became
14. were
15. commenced
16. are
17. pass
18. sealed
19. will book
20. marked
21. **Melissa:** indirect object; **song:** direct object
22. **me:** indirect object; **how:** direct object
23. **Jim:** indirect object; **omelet:** direct object
24. **picture:** direct object
25. **me:** indirect object; **piece:** direct object
26. **bananas:** direct object
27. **me:** indirect object; **card:** direct object
28. **people:** indirect object; **flyers:** direct object
29. **bruise:** direct object
30. **glasses:** direct object; **them:** direct object
31. predicate noun: **owner**; predicate adjective: none
32. predicate noun: **members**; predicate adjective: none
33. predicate noun: **sailor**; predicate adjective: none
34. predicate noun: **dogs**; predicate adjective: none
35. predicate noun: none; predicate adjective: **popular**

36. predicate noun: none; predicate adjective: **difficult**

37. predicate noun: **spaces**; predicate adjective: none

38. predicate noun: none; predicate adjective: **healthy**

39. predicate noun: **teacher**; predicate adjective: none

40. predicate noun: none; predicate adjective: **popular**

AGREEMENT

> To get the right word in the right place is a rare achievement.
> To condense the diffused light of a page of thought into the
> luminous flash of a single sentence, is worthy to rank as a
> prize composition just by itself.

—Mark Twain, American author and humorist (1835–1910)

LESSON SUMMARY

Agreement between subjects and verbs and between antecedents and their pronouns is essential. Learn whether to use a singular or plural verb with compound subjects and indefinite
pronouns.

Subject-Verb Agreement

Subjects and verbs must always be compatible in number and person. A singular subject—referring to only one person, place, or thing—must be coupled with a singular verb. Likewise, plural subjects—referring to more than one person, place, or thing—need a plural verb.

Singular:	*Shirley* **wants** to buy a new car. *Rex* usually **plays** catch with me.	She **is** shopping for one now. He **was** not feeling well today.
Plural:	*Trish* and *Dot* **run** errands together. *Sandy, Alexa,* and *I* **discuss** books.	They **are** at the supermarket. We **were** hoping to meet today.

Notice the endings of the singular and the plural verbs. Unlike nouns, third-person singular verbs end in *-s*, while the corresponding plural verbs do not.

Verbs move sentences along. We are able to tell *when* events happen simply by noting the verb tense in a sentence. Because many verbs are easily recognizable, they come across as exceptionally harsh to our ears if used improperly. This is especially true of the most widely used verb form in the English language, *be*. The following table shows how *be* is conjugated according to number, form, and person (singular/plural, first/second/third person).

	SUBJECT	PRESENT	PAST
First/S	I	am	was
Second/S and P	you	are	were
Third/S	he, she, it	is	was
First/P	we	are	were
Third/P	they	are	were

It is interesting to note that the conjugated forms of *be* don't include the word *be* itself. For reference, the nonparticipial forms of *be* are as follows: *am, is, are, was, were*.

That being said, it is not unusual to hear *be* used improperly as a verb in casual language. Remember this rule: *Be* **never** follows a subject in a sentence without a helping verb.

Incorrect:
I **be** taking the mail to the post office this morning.
They **be** cooking dinner, and we **be** washing the dishes.

Correct:
I **am** taking the mail to the post office this morning.
They **are** cooking dinner, and we **are** washing the dishes.

Practice
Identify the verb that correctly agrees with the subject in each sentence.

1. According to the itinerary, Sheila and I (arrive, arrives) in Copenhagen around 4:00.

2. We (be, are, is) planning to visit Jake's family for Thanksgiving, and mine for Hanukkah.

3. Sometimes on rainy Saturday afternoons, I (make, makes) popcorn and have a movie marathon at home.

4. The directions (tell, tells) you to unplug the power cord after the device has finished charging.

5. He and Elton (meet, meets) every Monday afternoon to have coffee and talk about Sunday's Patriots game.

TIP

Do not let long sentences confuse you. Verbs do not have to agree with words that come between the subject and verb. "Jamal, as well as his best friends Alec and Carlos, is auditioning for *American Idol*." The singular subject, *Jamal*, takes a singular verb, *is*.

Compound Subjects and Verbs

When two or more subjects share the same verb, you have what is called a **compound subject**. The conjunctions *and*, *or*, and *nor* are used to connect compound subjects.

Example:
Pink and black **are** traditional ballet colors.

When *and* is used, the subjects are looked at as equals, so the verb is plural. An exception to this rule is when the subjects are thought of as a single unit, like *spaghetti and meatballs* or *macaroni and cheese*.

When singular subjects are joined by *or* or *nor*, each subject is considered a separate unit, so the verb is *singular*. When plural subjects are joined by *or* or *nor*, the verb is *plural*, since each of the subjects is plural.

Singular:
Green or yellow squash **is** used in this recipe.
Neither the chair nor the table **has** any scratches.

Plural:
Coaches or managers **attend** the monthly team meetings.
Neither parents nor spectators **have** any interest in attending.

TIP

In a sentence with a singular and a plural subject, it may be hard to decide whether to use a singular or a plural verb. But the solution is simple: Whichever subject is mentioned last in the sentence, whether singular or plural, determines the correct verb to use:

Either *pancakes* or *cereal* **is** available for breakfast today.
Either *cereal* or *pancakes* **are** available for breakfast today.

Practice

Identify the verb that correctly completes the following sentences.

6. Some of us in the office (take, takes) the A train, while others take the F train.

7. Neither Joe nor Mary (like, likes) seafood, so they always get chicken or salads when we go to Arnold's Crab Shack.

8. Orange zest or lemon zest (work, works) in this recipe.

9. Both of you (is, are) being very rude.

10. Tyrone or Genevieve (meet, meets) with new clients to discuss their advertising needs.

Pronoun Subjects and Verbs

Indefinite pronouns, such as *everyone*, *both*, *few*, and *all*, are general when referring to people, places, or things. Because we are concerned with subjects and verbs agreeing in number, it is easy to tell if most indefinite pronouns are singular or plural, with only a handful of exceptions.

INDEFINITE PRONOUNS						
SINGULAR				PLURAL	BOTH	
anybody	everybody	neither	other	both	all	some
anyone	everyone	nobody	somebody	few	any	
anything	everything	no one	someone	many	more	
each	little	nothing	something	others	most	
either	much	one		several	none	

As with any other pronoun, a singular indefinite pronoun takes a singular verb, and a plural one takes a plural verb. When using pronouns that can be both singular and plural, you need to look at the noun being referred to by the indefinite pronoun to help you determine which verb to use:

> **Most** of these *peaches* **are** bruised.
> **Most** of his *room* **is** clean.

Practice

Identify the verb that will agree with the indefinite pronouns in the following sentences.

11. Most of us (is, are) not even from this town.

12. Anybody who (think, thinks) waiting tables is an easy job should spend an hour working at my restaurant.

13. Somebody (need, needs) to remind me when it's time to leave.

14. Everything (seem, seems) more fun when you have good company.

15. All of us (remember, remembers) that day when Clyde set the hamster loose in the classroom.

Antecedents and Pronouns

You studied pronouns in Lesson 3, but here are some additional pronouns you need to know.

COMMON ENGLISH PRONOUNS				
all	another	any	anybody	anyone
anything	both	each	either	everybody
everyone	everything	few	he	her
hers	herself	him	himself	his
I	it	its	itself	many
me	mine	my	myself	neither
no one	nobody	none	nothing	one
others	our	ours	ourselves	she
some	somebody	someone	something	that
their	theirs	them	themselves	these
they	this	us	we	what
which	who	whom	whose	you
your	yours	yourself	yourselves	

Without pronouns, communicating would be very contrived because of the necessary repetition of nouns.

Example:
Lillian and Gina went to Florida for a long weekend. Lillian and Gina planned to meet up with Lillian and Gina's old friends Stephanie and Jean. Lillian, Gina, Stephanie, and Jean decided Lillian, Gina, Stephanie, and Jean would have lunch at Lillian, Gina, Stephanie, and Jean's old watering hole. Lillian, Gina, Stephanie, and Jean had a great time, and Lillian and Gina decided to have lunch there with Stephanie and Jean again soon.

Luckily, pronouns can take the place of nouns and make a story less boring. The antecedent is the word the pronoun replaces.

Example:
Adel liked the new headphones she bought this afternoon.

The pronoun *she* refers to *Adel*, so *Adel* is the antecedent. Because *Adel* is one girl, *she* is used instead of *they*. There must be agreement of gender, number, and person between an antecedent and its pronoun.

	SINGULAR	PLURAL
First person:	I, me, my, mine	we, us, our
Second person:	you, your, yours	you, your, yours
Third person:	he, she, it	they, them, their

Let's see why that is not only important, but *necessary*:

Mrs. Parker shopped for a pair of strappy sandals in the perfect shade of chartreuse green and yellow for *his* new sundress.

It is obvious that Mrs. Parker is a female, so the only appropriate possessive pronoun to agree would be *her*, not *his* as in the sentence. Try another:

Rosemarie yawned and put *their* feet up to take *his* afternoon nap.

Rosemarie is tired and wants to take a nap, but the sentence has her putting other people's feet up and, unfortunately, taking someone else's nap for him.

When a sentence has multiple subjects, pronoun ambiguity sets in for listeners or readers. With too many *he*'s, *she*'s, and *they*'s, the message may become garbled, and the audience gets lost.

Example:
Kris told Nancy that Fran ran into Hali after she left class, and over coffee, she spilled the beans that she heard her boyfriend say that he thought she was boring.

That is confusing. Who left class? Hali, Fran, or Kris? Who spilled the beans? Kris? Perhaps Fran or Nancy? And whose boyfriend thinks who is boring?

TIP

A sentence may contain more than one noun/pronoun–verb pair. Make sure that each pair agrees in number.

Practice

Determine which pronoun best fits for pronoun-antecedent agreement in each sentence.

16. The members of the sales team are in danger of not making _____ numbers this quarter.

17. Andrew Stevens, the art critic, was notoriously difficult to please, so Alyssa was hesitant to show _____ her painting.

18. Many chose to have _____ pictures taken with the celebrity at the party.

19. The puppy wagged _____ tail whenever I walked into the room.

20. None of us remembered to turn the lights out before _____ left the house.

Answers

1. arrive
2. are
3. make
4. tell
5. meet
6. take
7. likes
8. works
9. are
10. meets
11. are
12. thinks
13. needs
14. seems
15. remember
16. their
17. him
18. their
19. its
20. we

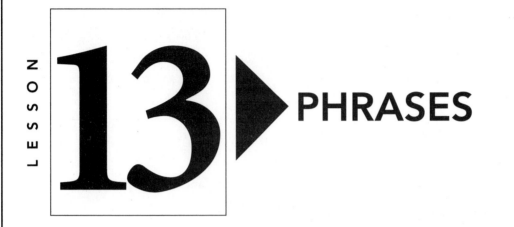

LESSON 13 ▶ PHRASES

The government's view of the economy could be summed up in a few short phrases: If it moves, tax it. If it keeps moving, regulate it. And if it stops moving, subsidize it.

—Ronald Reagan, U.S. Republican politician
and president (1911–2004)

LESSON SUMMARY

Did you know that in a sentence, a little group of words can wear many hats? Well, it can. In one sentence, it may act like an adjective; in another, it may be like an adverb; and in still another, it may function as a noun. Find out how all this happens in this lesson.

A phrase is a group of two or more words that makes sense, but not complete sense, because it does not have both a subject and a verb. The group of words that make up a phrase—and there are many kinds of phrases—is used as a single part of speech.

SAMPLE PHRASES	
NO PREDICATE	**NO SUBJECT**
The bicycles	goes skating often
Several	is from another planet
Our house	are missing some parts

In a sentence, a prepositional phrase can play the role of an adjective, in which case it is called an adjective phrase, or an adverb, in which case it is an adverb phrase. There are also verbal phrases (based on verbs) that can be participial phrases, gerund phrases, or infinitive phrases, and can function as nouns, adjectives, or adverbs. Lastly, appositive phrases explain or give more detail about the word or words they modify.

Prepositional Phrases

The **prepositional phrase** is the most common type of phrase. (For a review of prepositions, see Lesson 9.)

Adjective and Adverb Phrases

A prepositional phrase, which begins with a preposition and ends with a noun or pronoun, can function like an adjective or adverb in a sentence. Like an adjective, an adjective phrase answers *what kind?* or *which one?* about the noun or pronoun it modifies. Unlike an adjective, which typically precedes the noun it modifies, an adjective phrase generally comes after the noun.

> **Example:**
> A group of friends **from work** are meeting tonight for dinner.

Here, the prepositional phrase *from work* acts like an adjective. We know it is an adjective phrase because it modifies the noun *group* and answers the question *which one?* about the group.

Adverb phrases modify verbs, adjectives, and adverbs. An adverb phrase answers *where? when? how?* or *to what extent?* about the word it modifies, and usually provides more detail than a typical adverb.

> **Example:**
> We will meet **at our favorite restaurant at six o'clock**.

Here, the prepositional phrases *at our favorite restaurant* and *at six o'clock* act like adverbs, modifying the

verb *meet* and answering the questions *where?* and *when?* about the meeting.

> **TIP**
>
> Remember, a phrase is just a group of words. It may be a subject or a predicate, but it cannot be both. Therefore, it cannot stand alone as a sentence.

Practice

Identify the adjective and adverb phrases in the following sentences.

1. Forests with dry grass and brush burn easily.

2. The workers on the platform worked hard in the hot sun.

3. The picture in the antique frame was of my grandmother.

4. The gray squirrels scampered along the fence rail in the backyard.

5. The divers traversed through deep waters of the Caribbean.

Verbal Phrases

The three types of verbal phrases are participial phrases (which act like adjectives), infinitive phrases (which act like nouns, adjectives, or adverbs), and gerund phrases (which act like nouns).

Participial Phrases

Participial phrases begin with a participle—a present tense (*-ing*) verb or a past tense (*-ed, -en, -t,* or *-n*) verb. These phrases act like adjectives, describing or giving more detail about nouns or pronouns.

Examples:
Looking hot and tired, the gardener sat in the shade of a nearby tree.
Shaken by the unexpected accident, Harry called 911 for assistance.

The present participle *looking* (*look* + *ing*) modifies the noun *gardener*. The words *hot and tired* complete the participial phrase. The phrase *shaken by the unexpected accident* follows the same configuration, except it is in past participle (*shake* + *n*) form.

Infinitive Phrases

Infinitive phrases begin with the word *to* plus a verb. These phrases act like nouns, adjectives, or adverbs, depending on their function in the sentence.

> **Example:**
> **To run a mile in less than six minutes** was Tommy's aim this season.

The infinitive phrase *to run a mile in less than six minutes* is functioning as a noun because it is the complete subject of the sentence.

> **Example:**
> Tommy aims **to run a mile in less than six minutes** this season.

In this sentence, *to run a mile in less than six minutes* also functions as a noun because it is the direct object of the verb *aims*.

> **Example:**
> **To run a mile in less than six minutes**, Tommy trains hard this season.

Here, *to run a mile in less than six minutes* functions as an *adjective* because it modifies the noun *Tommy*.

> **Example:**
> Tommy is training this season **to run a mile in less than six minutes**.

Now, *to run a mile in less than six minutes* functions as an adverb modifying the verb *training*.

Gerund Phrases

Gerund phrases begin with a gerund—an *-ing* verb acting as a noun. Gerund phrases always work like a noun in a sentence, so they can function as either subjects or objects.

> **Example:**
> **Tasting chocolate for a living** can be a delicious yet fattening profession.

The gerund phrase *tasting chocolate for a living* functions as a noun and is the complete subject of the sentence.

> **Example:**
> Debbie's profession is **sampling chocolate**.

The gerund phrase *sampling chocolate* functions as a noun and is the subject complement of the linking verb *is* and the subject *profession*.

> **Example:**
> Debbie enjoys **working with chocolate**.

The gerund phrase *working with chocolate* functions as a noun and is the direct object of the verb *enjoys*.

Practice

Identify the types of phrases that are italicized in the following sentences.

6. *To conclude tonight's program*, our chief of staff would like to say a few words.

7. *Wanting to save money*, Lysbeth spent the morning clipping and filing coupons.

8. Marybeth dreams about *becoming a NASA astronaut.*

9. The plumber was unable *to finish the difficult job* in one day.

10. *Excusing the boys* for their rude and reckless behavior was not an option.

Appositive Phrases

An **appositive phrase** renames, identifies, or gives more detail about a noun or pronoun that it follows in a sentence.

Example:
My brother, **a clown by profession**, works all weekend at parties and gatherings.

In this sentence, the noun *brother* is being further identified by the appositive phrase *a clown by profession.*

TIP

Since it tells more about a noun, you can omit an appositive phrase without losing the basic idea of a sentence. In the previous sentence, drop the phrase, and you still know the brother works weekends at social gatherings.

Practice

Identify the appositive phrases in each sentence and the noun or pronoun it modifies.

11. Julie, an excellent tennis player, will be going to the state finals for the Junior American Tennis Association this August.

12. The peanut, not really a nut but a legume, is a major allergen for children and adults around the world.

13. *Pygmalion* is by George Bernard Shaw, one of my favorite playwrights.

14. To play the marimba, a musical instrument in the percussion family, Carlo used small wooden mallets.

15. Agatha Christie's *Ten Little Indians*, a classic mystery, was first published in the United States in 1940.

Answers

1. **with dry grass and brush:** adjective phrase
2. **on the platform:** adjective phrase; **in the hot sun:** adverb phrase
3. **in the antique frame, of my grandmother:** adjective phrases
4. **along the fence rail, in the backyard:** adverb phrases
5. **through deep waters:** adverb phrase; **of the Caribbean:** adjective phrase
6. infinitive phrase
7. participial phrase
8. gerund phrase
9. infinitive phrase
10. gerund phrase
11. **an excellent tennis player** modifies *Julie*
12. **not really a nut but a legume** modifies *peanut*
13. **one of my favorite playwrights** modifies *George Bernard Shaw*
14. **a musical instrument in the percussion family** modifies *marimba*
15. **a classic mystery** modifies *Ten Little Indians*

14 ▶ CLAUSES

The most emphatic place in a clause or sentence is the end.
This is the climax; and, during the momentary pause that
follows, that last word continues, as it were, to reverberate in
the reader's mind. It has, in fact, the last word.

—Frank Laurence Lucas, English literary critic,
poet, novelist, and playwright (1894–1967)

LESSON SUMMARY

Like phrases, clauses are parts of speech that can take on many
different jobs—they can even function as stand-alone sentences.
Find out why and how in this lesson.

A **clause** is also a group of words, but it differs from a phrase in that it has its own subject and verb.
Therefore, some clauses function as sentences, either independently or within a larger sentence.
One sentence might contain, or even be entirely composed of, as many as three or more clauses.
The sentence would be a combination of two possible kinds of clauses, **independent** and **subordinate**.

Independent Clauses

Sometimes referred to as a main clause, an **independent clause** can stand alone as a simple sentence.

Examples:
You have a nice smile.
It lights up your eyes.

With the help of a semicolon or a coordinating conjunction, we can join these two independent clauses to form a single sentence.

Examples:
You have a nice smile; it lights up your eyes.
You have a nice smile, **and** it lights up your eyes.

Don't confuse the comma with the semicolon. Joining the two clauses with a comma instead of a semicolon would result in what is called a comma splice. (See Lesson 18.)

Examples:
I looked for my lost address book, **but** I could not find it.
Charlotte watered the tree every day, **for** it was new.
Hans wanted to learn to play golf, **so** he took lessons.

As mentioned before, some sentences may contain as many as three or more independent clauses.

Example:
I looked for my lost address book, **but** I could not find it, **so** I decided to start a new one; I knew it would be useful.

Subordinate Clauses

A **subordinate clause**, or **dependent clause**, also contains a subject and verb, but it cannot stand alone as a simple sentence. It depends on another clause in the sentence to help it do its job. Subordinate clauses look like independent clauses, but they can begin with subordinating conjunctions.

Examples:
before I knew it
so I don't forget it
whenever you're in town

SUBORDINATING CONJUNCTIONS				
after	although	as if	as long as	as much as
because	before	even if	even though	if
in order that	now that	only if	since	so
so long as	though	unless	until	when
whenever	whereas	whether	while	where

Subordinate clauses can also begin with relative pronouns.

Examples:
whom I saw earlier
whose name I forget
whichever comes first

RELATIVE PRONOUNS			
that	which	whichever	who
whoever	whose	whom	whomever

When attaching a subordinate clause to the front of a main, or independent, clause, it is necessary to use a comma between the two clauses.

Example:
Before I knew it, I was being lambasted by the angry sergeant for my comment.

When attaching a clause to the end of a main clause, no comma is needed.

Example:
Put your name and number on the card **so I don't forget it.**

Practice
Determine whether the group of words is an independent or a subordinate clause.

1. Did you know

2. He made it

3. According to Artie

4. Remember your manners

5. If you go to Paris after all

6. He said he'd had enough

7. Starting with Jamie

8. Henry's hobby of collecting stamps

9. I appreciate the gesture

10. Because he liked pickles

Subordinate clauses can function as three different parts of speech: a *noun*, an *adjective*, or an *adverb*.

Noun Clauses
We know that nouns can play many roles. They can be subjects, predicate nominatives, direct objects, appositives, indirect objects, or objects of prepositions. Some words that begin noun clauses are question-starters like *who, what, where, when, why, how,* as well as the words *that, whether, whom, whoever,* and *whomever.*

Example:
I see Robin.

Here, the proper noun *Robin* is the direct object of *see.*

Example:
I see that Robin finished three books already.

The noun clause *that Robin finished three books already* functions as the direct object of the verb *see.*

Example:
Charles, a local hero, received an award.

The phrase *a local hero* is an appositive phrase that modifies the noun *Charles.*

Example:
Charles, who is a local hero, received an award.

The clause *who is a local hero* is a noun clause functioning as an appositive.

Practice

Identify the noun clause in each of the following sentences.

11. Our choice depends on whether he is the only one we know at that company.

12. That she never gets sunburn is not an excuse to skip using sunblock.

13. The school will announce that Mrs. Bloomfeld, a teacher for almost 50 years, is retiring this year.

14. I don't understand what you want me to do with this.

15. How she will make the finals is Betty's main goal at this swim meet.

16. What she's planning to do for the talent show is a big secret.

17. You should know what to do if there's ever a fire in your home.

18. Whether you want to go doesn't matter; we have a 2:00 appointment.

19. The responsibility for making coffee goes to whoever wakes up first.

20. That we stop at the grocery store before we go to the beach was a good idea.

Adjective Clauses

Subordinate clauses function as adjectives when they describe or modify nouns or pronouns. Like adjectives, they answer the questions *what kind?* and *which one?* about the words they modify. An **adjective clause** begins with a word like the relative pronouns *who, whose, whom, that,* or *which,* or the subordinating conjunctions *where* or *when.*

Example:
The painting, which had a price tag of $10,000, was too expensive.

The adjective clause *which had a price tag of $10,000* is modifying the noun *painting.*

Example:
The man who witnessed the robbery was later interviewed by the newspaper.

The adjective clause *who witnessed the robbery* modifies the noun *man.*

Practice

Identify the adjective clause in each sentence.

21. Marty grabbed the lunch that was on the counter, even though it was clearly marked with Eleanor's name.

22. I'm looking for someone who shares my interests.

23. I like to pick out the red candies that are cherry flavored.

24. At the end of the hall, the door that is on the right is the one you want.

25. Do you remember that time when we stayed up all night and watched scary movies?

26. I can make it to the 7:00 showing, which is a double feature.

27. Michelle wanted to find a place that was quiet enough to let her finish studying.

28. Benji hurt his wrist falling off the old swing that is in the backyard.

29. At the animal shelter, Donna decided to adopt the cat that has one eye.

30. We're interested in buying that house that is on the corner of Maple Drive and Windsor Place.

Adverb Clauses

When a subordinate clause answers *where*, *when*, *how*, or *why*, it is functioning as an adverb and is called an **adverb clause**. Like other adverbs, the adverb clause answers *where? when? why?* and *how?* about the verb, adjective, or other adverb it modifies. Adverb clauses begin with subordinating conjunctions such as *because*, *although*, *once*, *until*, and *after*, to name a few.

Example:
As he set the cup down, coffee spilled all over his shoe.

The adverb clause *as he set the cup down* modifies the verb *spilled*.

Example:
Allison played the piano longer than David did.

The adverb clause *than David did* modifies the adverb *longer*.

TIP

Because adverb clauses tell why something in the main clause happened, you will find them in cause-and-effect text and questions on tests. And since adverb clauses show differences, they are also used in compare-and-contrast items.

Practice

Identify the adverb clause in each of the following sentences.

31. Because she had a terrible sunburn, she decided not to go to the beach.

32. Elena was not the class valedictorian, even though she had a near-perfect GPA.

33. If you want to heal faster, you should be careful to stay off your sprained ankle.

34. My dog is happy to see me whenever I walk through the door.

35. Mike is usually very grouchy before he has his first cup of coffee each morning.

36. If you're stopping at the grocery store after you finish working, please pick up some milk.

37. Even if he worked extra hours, Brian calculated that it would still take him six months to save up for a new car.

38. In our competition to see who could give up drinking soda longer, Mary Ellen lasted longer than I did.

39. Erica enjoyed the movie, although she thought the book was better.

40. As we got ready to go to bed, the baby woke and started crying.

Answers

1. subordinate clause
2. independent clause
3. subordinate clause
4. independent clause
5. subordinate clause
6. independent clause
7. subordinate clause
8. subordinate clause
9. independent clause
10. subordinate clause
11. whether he is the only one we know
12. that she never gets sunburn
13. that Mrs. Bloomfeld, a teacher for almost 50 years, is retiring
14. what you want me to do
15. how she will make the finals
16. what she's planning to do
17. what to do
18. whether you want to go
19. whoever wakes up first
20. that we stop at the grocery store
21. that was on the counter
22. who shares my interests
23. that are cherry flavored
24. that is on the right
25. when we stayed up all night
26. which is a double feature
27. that was quiet enough
28. that is in the backyard
29. that has one eye
30. that is on the corner of Maple Drive and Windsor Place
31. Because she had a terrible sunburn
32. even though she had a near-perfect GPA
33. If you want to heal faster
34. whenever I walk through the door
35. before he has his first cup of coffee
36. after you finish working
37. Even if he worked extra hours
38. than I did
39. although she thought the book was better
40. As we got ready to go to bed

15 ▶ CONJUNCTIONS

First, it [clarity] involves the use of normal words, secondly the use of connectives. Sentences which are unconnected and disjointed throughout are always unclear. For the beginning of each clause is obscured by the lack of connectives. . . .

—Demetrius of Phaleron, Greek orator, statesman,
and teacher of rhetoric (350 BCE–280 BCE)

LESSON SUMMARY

When you write, does it matter if your connectors are correlative, coordinating, or subordinating? Does it matter if the elements being connected are similar? Find out here.

Conjunctions are connecting words. They join words, phrases, and sentences in writing and speech. Conjunctions come in three forms: *coordinating, correlative,* and *subordinating.* Coordinating and correlative conjunctions connect similar elements: nouns with nouns, phrases with phrases, sentences with sentences. Subordinating conjunctions connect elements that are dissimilar.

> ### TIP
>
> Some people think it is wrong to start a sentence with a conjunction like *and*, *but*, or *so*. Today, it is perfectly acceptable and helps to add emphasis. Just don't overdo it.

Coordinating Conjunctions

The acronym FANBOYS will help you remember the seven, and *only* seven, **coordinating conjunctions**: *for, and, nor, but, or, yet,* and *so.*

COORDINATING CONJUNCTIONS	
for Connecting sentences:	expresses a logical relationship, where one element is the cause of another Alice sold her condominium, for she wanted a house.
and Connecting phrases:	joins elements that are equal in importance June vacuumed the floors and dusted the furniture.
nor Connecting words:	presents an alternate idea or thought He was so nervous he could neither eat nor sleep.
but Connecting words:	indicates a difference or exception between elements Their vacation was short but enjoyable.
or Connecting words:	presents an alternative or option for an element of equal importance You can have juice or soda with your meal.
yet Connecting phrases:	joins elements that follow logically but are opposing She is so glamorous yet down to earth.
so Connecting sentences:	suggests the consequence of related ideas *Marge cut the grass yesterday, so she got to relax today.*

Practice

In each of the following sentences, identify the coordinating conjunction and the words or groups of words it is connecting.

1. I thought the movie was sophisticated, yet easy to follow.

2. Kelly or Roger is responsible for cleaning up after the puppy.

3. This tea is supposed to help relieve cold symptoms, but I haven't noticed a difference.

4. She's not sure if she wants to go to the University of Connecticut or Wesleyan University.

5. Neither Jason nor I feel like going to the party, but we promised Stacy we'd be there.

6. Tim had to make a trip to the store, for we were out of soap and bread.

7. Andrew has already agreed to paint the scenery, so I will need you or Maureen to organize the props.

8. I knew it was supposed to rain, yet I neglected to bring my umbrella.

9. He knows the show starts at 8:00, so he has planned to pick us up at 7:30.

10. Her New Year's resolution is to lose weight, and she has joined a gym to get started.

Correlative Conjunctions

Correlative conjunctions come in pairs and are used as such. They connect sentence elements of similar structure and importance. There are five common pairs of correlative conjunctions.

CORRELATIVE CONJUNCTIONS	
both . . . and	Both *Kelly* and *Ingrid* attended the cooking demonstration.
either . . . or	Either *you let him go* or *I'm calling the police.*
neither . . . nor	I can neither *go shopping* nor *go to the movies* because the mall is closed.
not only . . . but also	We spent not only *the summer* but also *the fall in Alaska.*
whether . . . or	Sometimes I don't know whether *Lynn* or *Jill* should take the lead.

Practice
Insert acceptable correlative conjunctions into the following sentences.

11. _____ Eileen _____ Marjorie needs to confirm how many chairs we'll need.

12. _____ English _____ math are my favorite subjects.

13. _____ Henry _____ Veronica wants to go to St. Louis—they'd rather go to Chicago instead.

14. I can't decide _____ I should bring Julie _____ Kerry as my date to the dance.

15. Greg thinks that we can _____ finish the project _____ have time to get started on the next one before Thursday.

16. My list of chores from _____ Mom _____ Dad is getting too long.

17. _____ does Dionne have the highest grade in the class, _____ she also completed the extra credit assignment.

18. _____ Italian food _____ Chinese food sounds good to me right now.

19. _____ you have prepared _____ not, the test is on Wednesday morning.

20. _____ you want to go _____ you don't.

TIP

As you read, you may find that *whether* is used without its pair-mate, which can be okay. For example, "I'm not sure *whether* I can go with you." Here, the other half of the pair is implied: "I'm not sure *whether* (*or not*) I can go with you."

Subordinating Conjunctions

Subordinating conjunctions connect an independent clause to a dependent, or subordinate, clause. For a review of clauses, see Lesson 14. The subordinating conjunction expresses the relationship between the meanings of the independent and dependent clauses.

SUBORDINATING CONJUNCTIONS			
TIME	**CAUSE/EFFECT**	**CONDITION**	**CONTRAST**
after	because	as long as	although
before	so	unless	even though
when	now that	provided that	though
since	in order that	so long as	as much as
until	as if	if	while
as soon as		whether	whereas
whenever			even if

The preceding table shows some commonly used subordinating conjunctions and some relationships they convey. The logic of their use lies in the relationship of the dependent and subordinate clauses. For example, consider this sentence:

> The program will have to be discontinued unless more interest is generated.

Here the clause *unless more interest is generated* cannot stand alone because its meaning depends on the independent clause *The program will have to be discontinued.*

TIP

Think you're seeing things? You're not; many subordinating conjunctions previously shown are also listed as prepositions in Lesson 9. Don't forget—words can play many different roles in a sentence! For example, depending on its function, the word *since* can play three roles. It can be an adverb:

> He's been over there ever *since*.

or a preposition:

> I haven't had fresh pineapple *since* my trip to Hawaii.

or a conjunction:

> We haven't been to the beach *since* the weather has been so unpleasant all summer.

Practice

Using the table on page 124 for reference, create a new sentence with the clauses and a subordinating conjunction.

21. The *Twilight* books are so popular. Vampire romance books are everywhere.

22. I shoveled the driveway an hour ago. The snow is piling up again.

23. The pie was a little burned. It still tasted good.

24. We can't make it out to Colorado for the conference. We plan to call in for the board meeting.

25. You don't have anything to do. You can start going through the books in that box.

Answers

1. sophisticated, **yet** easy to follow
2. Kelly **or** Roger
3. This tea is supposed to help relieve cold symptoms, **but** I haven't noticed a difference.
4. University of Connecticut **or** Wesleyan University
5. Jason **nor** I
6. Tim had to make a trip to the store, **for** we were out of soap and bread.
7. Andrew has already agreed to paint the scenery, **so** I will need you or Maureen to organize the props.
8. I knew it was supposed to rain, **yet** I neglected to bring my umbrella.
9. He knows the show starts at 8:00, **so** he has planned to pick us up at 7:30.
10. Her New Year's resolution is to lose weight, **and** she has joined a gym to get started.
11. Either . . . or
12. Both . . . and
13. Neither . . . nor
14. whether . . . or
15. both . . . and
16. both . . . and
17. Not only . . . but
18. Either . . . or/Neither . . . nor
19. Whether . . . or
20. Either . . . or
21. *Because* the *Twilight* books are so popular, vampire romance books are everywhere.
    Now that the *Twilight* books are so popular, vampire romance books are everywhere.
22. *Even though* I shoveled the driveway an hour ago, the snow is piling up again.
    After I shoveled the driveway an hour ago, the snow is piling up again.
23. *Even though* the pie was a little burned, it still tasted good.
    Even if the pie was a little burned, it still tasted good.

24. *Because* we can't make it out to Colorado for the conference, we plan to call in for the board meeting.

Even though we can't make it out to Colorado for the conference, we plan to call in for the board meeting.

25. *If* you don't have anything to do, you can start going through the books in that box.

Now that you don't have anything to do, you can start going through the books in that box.

16 ▶ COMBINING SENTENCES

It is my ambition to say in ten sentences what others say in a whole book.

—Friedrich Nietzsche, German philosopher
and writer (1844–1900)

LESSON SUMMARY

Good writing involves sentences of varying lengths and complexities that make text more appealing and inviting to readers. To start with, you can achieve this by combining your sentences. In this lesson, you will learn how to do just that.

I f you have ever read a book written for young readers, you probably noticed that the sentences were simple, direct, and short. While that kind of language may be helpful for beginning readers, it becomes extremely monotonous and uninteresting for advanced readers. Books that are more interesting to read contain a variety of sentence lengths and complexities. Authors accomplish this by combining sentences.

Besides simple sentences, there are three other kinds of basic sentences: compound, complex, and compound-complex.

We know that independent clauses are **simple sentences**, which must have, minimally, a simple subject and predicate. (See Lesson 11.)

Examples:
Nathan talks.
Les listens.
Nora laughs.

The following table maps out simple sentence structures. These examples do not include the infinite number of modifying words, phrases, and clauses that could be added for detail.

SIMPLE SENTENCE STRUCTURES	
(Implied subject you) + (**V**)erb = simple sentence	*Watch!*
(**S**)ubject + **V** = simple sentence	*Sam watched.*
S + **V** + (**O**)bject =	*Sam watched baseball.*
(**C**)ompound **S** + **V** + **O** =	*Sam and Joe watched baseball.*
S + **CV** + **O** =	*Sam watched and played baseball.*
S + **V** + **CO** =	*Sam watched baseball and football.*
CS + **CV** + **O** =	*Sam and Joe watched and played baseball.*
CS + **V** + **CO** =	*Sam and Joe watched baseball and football.*
S + **CV** + **CO** =	*Sam watched and played baseball and football.*
CS + **CV** + **CO** =	**Sam and Joe watched and played baseball and football.**

Compound Sentences

Shorter sentences can be combined into one complete thought or sentence.

Example:
Nathan, Les, and Nora enjoy talking, listening, and laughing.

While that livens up the writing a bit, it is still rather limited. For more complex sentence structure, take two or more related sentences, or independent clauses, and join them with a coordinating conjunction (*for*, *and*, *nor*, *but*, *or*, *yet*, or *so*) or a semicolon to create a **compound sentence**.

Examples:
Nathan and Nora talk and laugh; Les listens.
Les listens; Nathan and Nora talk and laugh.
Nathan and Nora talk and laugh, **but** Les listens.
Les listens, **yet** Nathan and Nora talk and laugh.
Nathan and Nora talk and laugh, **so** Les listens.
Les listens, **and** Nathan and Nora talk and laugh.

The combinations are, of course, interchangeable. The coordinating conjunction *or* is a good choice if the equal subjects have an alternative. The coordinating conjunction *nor* is a better choice if the expressions are negative. The conjunction *for*, denoting "because," would work grammatically, but isn't very logical in this case.

Practice

Combine the following simple sentences to create a compound sentence.

1. My bag was already packed. I realized I should pack extra socks as well.

2. I decided to visit London on vacation. I renewed my passport in anticipation.

3. She really likes cats. She's allergic to them.

4. The grocery store on Sandy Street was out of avocados. I found some at the farmer's market in Dempsey Park.

5. The power went out. We had no idea how long the outage would last.

6. Mark went to the concert Saturday night. Felix went too.

7. The emerald is my birthstone. I prefer pearl jewelry.

8. Jill bought her mom a book for her birthday. Melissa bought her flowers. Brian bought her a gift card for her favorite restaurant.

9. The comedy show was hilarious. I plan to bring my friends with me to the next one.

10. We wanted to celebrate our anniversary. We went out to dinner.

Complex Sentences

In addition to compound sentences, we can create **complex sentences** by combining one independent clause and one or more subordinate (dependent) clauses.

Examples:
Les sat and listened *while Nathan and Nora laughed and talked.*
While Nathan and Nora laughed and talked, Les sat and listened.
Les sat and listened *while Nathan and Nora laughed and talked, although he wasn't feeling well.*
Although he wasn't feeling well, Les sat and listened *while Nathan and Nora laughed and talked.*

TIP

Remember to put your key message in the main subject/verb position of your sentence. Do not hide it in other clauses.

Compound-Complex Sentences

Finally, we can create **compound-complex sentences**, using at least two independent clauses and one or more subordinate clauses.

Examples:
Les sat and listened *while Nathan and Nora laughed and talked,* **for** he wasn't feeling well.
While Nathan and Nora laughed and talked, Les sat and listened, **for** he wasn't feeling well.
Les wasn't feeling well, **so** he sat and listened *while Nathan and Nora laughed and talked.*

Note that the boldfaced word in each of these sentences is a conjunction.

Practice

Identify the independent and subordinate clauses in the following sentences and determine whether they are complex or compound-complex.

11. If you want to go with me to the library, you will need to be ready to leave in about ten minutes.

12. Because Sandra had nowhere else to be until 7:00, she ran errands around town and was able to fit in a yoga class.

13. Although the meteorologist predicted that the storm would miss us, we put out the snow shovels anyway, and Jerry salted the sidewalk in front of our house just in case.

14. Because she was confident, Liz thought she could do it on her own, but she was grateful when Myles offered to help.

15. Fred spent the afternoon cleaning out the garage, and he was pleased to find his old vinyl record collection, which he thought had been thrown out years ago.

16. I enjoyed the book, but I didn't care for the movie, which changed everything except the characters' names.

17. When he volunteered at the senior center, Kevin made a lot of friends, and he learned to love playing Scrabble.

18. If you want to lower your cholesterol, doctors advise exercising more and eating better.

19. The watercress salad was disappointing, but the chicken entrée was fantastic, with its crisp skin and fresh herbs.

20. After I hit the snooze button about six times, it was inevitable that I would be late to work.

Appositive Phrases

By adding modifiers in the form of adjectives, adverbs, or phrases to any type of sentence, we can make it even more interesting:

Nathan and Nora, **best friends**, talked and laughed **about last night's party**, but Les, **who wasn't feeling well**, just sat **quietly** and listened.

The appositive phrase *best friends*, the adverb phrase *about last night's party*, the noun clause *who wasn't feeling well*, and the adverb *quietly* were added to the sentences to provide more information about the subjects *Nathan*, *Nora*, and *Les*, and the predicates *laughed*, *talked*, and *sat*. Vivid details such as these make sentences more attention grabbing and inviting to read.

> **TIP**
>
> When you write, read your more complex sentences aloud, and then make changes until you find the smoothest, most effective combinations.

Answers

(Possible answers are shown.)

1. My bag was already packed, **but** I realized I should pack extra socks as well.

2. I decided to visit London on vacation, **so** I renewed my passport in anticipation.

3. She really likes cats, **but** she's allergic to them.

4. The grocery store on Sandy Street was out of avocados, **but** I found some at the farmer's market in Dempsey Park.

5. The power went out, **and** we had no idea how long the outage would last.

6. Mark went to the concert on Saturday night, **and** Felix went too.

7. The emerald is my birthstone, **yet** I prefer pearl jewelry.

8. Jill bought her mom a book for her birthday, Melissa bought her flowers, **and** Brian bought her a gift card for her favorite restaurant.

9. The comedy show was hilarious, **so** I plan to bring my friends with me to the next one.

10. We went out to dinner, **for** we wanted to celebrate our anniversary.

11. If you want to go with me to the library [subordinate clause], you will need to be ready to leave in about ten minutes [independent clause]. (complex)

12. Because Sandra had nowhere else to be until 7:00 [subordinate clause], she ran errands around town and was able to fit in a yoga class [independent clause]. (complex)

13. Although the meteorologist predicted that the storm would miss us [subordinate clause], we put out the snow shovels anyway [independent clause], and Jerry salted the sidewalk in front of our house just in case [independent clause]. (compound-complex)

14. Because she was confident [subordinate clause], Liz thought she could do it on her own [independent clause], but she was grateful when Myles offered to help [independent clause]. (compound-complex)

15. Fred spent the afternoon cleaning out the garage [independent clause], and he was pleased to find his old vinyl record collection [independent clause], which he thought had been thrown out years ago [subordinate clause]. (compound-complex)

16. I enjoyed the book [independent clause], but I didn't care for the movie [independent clause], which changed everything except the characters' names [subordinate clause]. (compound-complex)

17. When he volunteered at the senior center [subordinate clause], Kevin made a lot of friends [independent clause], and he learned to love playing Scrabble [independent clause]. (compound-complex)

18. If you want to lower your cholesterol [subordinate clause], doctors advise exercising more and eating better [independent clause]. (complex)

19. The watercress salad was disappointing [independent clause], but the chicken entrée was fantastic, with its crisp skin and fresh herbs [independent clause]. (compound)

20. After I hit the snooze button about six times [subordinate clause], it was inevitable that I would be late to work [independent clause]. (complex)

PUNCTUATION

17 ▶ END PUNCTUATION

My attitude toward punctuation is that it ought to be as conventional as possible.

—Ernest Hemingway, American author (1899–1961)

LESSON SUMMARY
Review the basics of end punctuation and its proper placement in sentences and abbreviations.

Periods

The most common form of end punctuation, the **period** (.) indicates the end of declarative sentences (statements of facts) and imperative sentences (simple commands or requests).

Examples:
Friday night is pizza night for my family**.**
Order an extra-large pepperoni with mushrooms, please**.**

Periods are also used with common abbreviations, such as months, days, and measurements (Dec., Mon., .02). Note that periods are **not** used for acronyms—abbreviations that use all capital letters (NATO, CEO, DNA) or for postal state abbreviations (SD, AL, NJ). Finally, periods are used after a person's initials (T.S. Eliot, W.C. Fields) and for titles such as Dr., Mr., or Gov. If a sentence ends with an abbreviation that has an end period, use it as the end mark, unless the sentence needs an exclamation point or question mark.

Example:
It happened at exactly 3 P.M.

But:
It happened at exactly 3 P.M.!
Did it happen at exactly 3 P.M.?

> ### TIP
>
> Always identify an acronym before you use it unless you are sure the average reader would know it because it is used more often than the words it stands for, such as AIDS or NATO. For example, you might write about the Federal Bureau of Investigation (FBI).

Practice

Insert periods to correctly punctuate each of the following sentences. You may check your answers against the key at the end of the lesson.

1. Mrs Sanderson checked her PO box, and was disappointed that she hadn't received her updated passport from the US government

2. I got up at 5 AM this morning, and am very tired as a result

3. The great showman PT Barnum once said, "There's a sucker born every minute"

4. Mr Dunphy was excited about visiting Washington DC for the first time since he was a kid

5. When she graduated from law school, she was able to add "JD" and "Esq" to her name on official documents

Question Marks

The **question mark** (?) indicates the end of an interrogatory sentence (direct question).

Examples:
Isn't this difficult?
May I try this time?
Are you okay?

> Indirect questions are statements that only sound like questions, so they end with a period.
>
> **Example:**
> She saw the frustrated look on my face and asked if she could help me. I asked her where the laundry detergent was.

Exclamation Points

An **exclamation point** (!) at the end of a sentence indicates strong feelings or authoritative commands. Interjections—free-standing words or phrases that express strong feelings—are also punctuated with exclamation points.

Examples:
Wow! What a mess you've made!
Look where you're going!

> ### TIP
>
> Using two or more exclamation points at the end of a sentence for extra emphasis may seem like a good idea, but in fact it is incorrect and may be thought of as rude.

Practice

Insert question marks, exclamation points, and periods to correctly punctuate each of the following sentences.

6. "Congratulations" she exclaimed, adding, "I hope you have many joyful years together"

7. "Can you let me know where to find Dr Simmons's office" Michael asked

8. Did you know that M Night Shyamalan has a new movie coming out next week

9. Her favorite morning show is *How Are You, San Francisco*

10. Help I am going to drop all of these groceries

Answers

1. Mrs. Sanderson checked her P.O. box, and was disappointed that she hadn't received her updated passport from the U.S. government.

2. I got up at 5 A.M. this morning, and am very tired as a result.

3. The great showman P.T. Barnum once said, "There's a sucker born every minute."

4. Mr. Dunphy was excited about visiting Washington, D.C., for the first time since he was a kid.

5. When she graduated from law school, she was able to add "J.D." and "Esq." to her name on official documents.

6. "Congratulations!" she exclaimed, adding, "I hope you have many joyful years together."

7. "Can you let me know where to find Dr. Simmons's office?" Michael asked.

8. Did you know that M. Night Shyamalan has a new movie coming out next week?

9. Her favorite morning show is *How Are You, San Francisco?*

10. Help! I am going to drop all of these groceries!

18 ▶ INTERNAL PUNCTUATION I

The writer who neglects punctuation, or mispunctuates, is liable to be misunderstood. . . . For the want of merely a comma, it often occurs that an axiom appears a paradox, or that a sarcasm is converted into a sermonoid.

—Edgar Allan Poe, American poet, critic, and short-story author (1809–1845)

LESSON SUMMARY

Commas, colons, and semicolons: They are ordinary kinds of punctuation, but they can be tricky. Learn where and when it is appropriate, and necessary, to use these misused marks.

Commas

You find **commas** everywhere. They indicate a pause in writing, just as taking a breath is a pause in speaking. Commas are used to set apart some modifiers, phrases, and clauses, and to enhance clarity by adding a sense of pace in written materials. There are some hard-and-fast rules for comma placement, but usage can often be a matter of personal style. Some writers use them frequently, and others do not. Just keep this in mind as you write: Too many, or too few, commas can obscure the meaning of your message. On the following pages, you'll find some basic rules about comma use.

Rule 1. Use commas to separate a series of three or more words, phrases, or clauses in a sentence.

> **Examples:**
> Please pick up **milk, bread,** and **bananas** from the store on your way home from work.
> Shelly **grabbed her coat, put it on,** and **ran to the bus**.

However, if your series uses the words *and* or *or* to connect the elements, then a comma is not necessary.

> **Examples:**
> Red **and** white **and** blue are patriotic colors.
> I cannot look at pictures of snakes **or** spiders **or** mice without anxiety.
>
> **Not:**
> Red**, and** white**, and** blue are patriotic colors.
> I cannot look at pictures of snakes**, or** spiders**, or** mice without anxiety.

If you use two or more adjectives to describe a noun or pronoun, use a comma to separate them.

> **Example:**
> He was a **happy, intelligent** child.

Be careful not to put a comma between the final adjective and the word it modifies.

Rule 2. Set off an introductory word or phrase from the rest of the sentence with a comma. (See Lesson 13 for a review of phrases.)

This pause stops readers from carrying the meaning of the introduction into the main part of the sentence, which might lead to misinterpretation.

> **Confusing:**
> After eating the flower shop owner and his manager tallied the day's receipts.

It seems as though someone was very hungry. . . .

> **Less Confusing:**
> After eating, the flower shop owner and his manager tallied the day's receipts.

> **Confusing:**
> Laughing Larry tried to tell the joke but just couldn't.

What a strange name, Laughing Larry. . . .

> **Less Confusing:**
> Laughing, Larry tried to tell the joke but just couldn't.

A transitional phrase should also be set off by a comma if it introduces a sentence, or by two commas if it is within the sentence.

> **Examples:**
> Fluke has two eyes on its left side and is**, in fact,** known as summer flounder.
> **On the other hand,** winter flounder has two eyes on its right side.

Rule 3. An appositive, a word or phrase that renames or enhances a noun, should be set off from the rest of the sentence by commas.

> **Examples:**
> You, **Nancy,** are the winner.
> Our neighbor, **a well-known architect,** helped us draw up the plans.
> **An experienced sailor,** Marie was unconcerned about the high waves.

These appositive phrases set off by commas are nonrestrictive, or not essential; even if they are removed, the sentence will remain complete.

Rule 4. Use commas in dates, in addresses, and in non-business letter salutations and closings.

Dates

Use commas after the day of the week, the day of the month, and after the year (only if the sentence continues):

> Our Cirque du Soleil tickets are for Wednesday, July 18, at Madison Square Garden in New York, NY.

TIP

If you are writing only the day and month or the month and year in a sentence, no comma is necessary.

Examples:
The Cirque du Soleil show was on July 18. The last time I saw a circus was in June 2007.

Addresses

When writing an address on an envelope or at the head of a letter, use a comma only before an apartment number or state abbreviation.

Example:

Marshall Grates
122 Ridge Road, Apt. 10
Ulysses Junction, MN 57231

When referring to an address within a sentence, use additional commas to substitute for line breaks.

Example:

Please send the order to Marshall Grates, 122 Ridge Road, Apt. 10, Ulysses Junction, MN 57231.

Notice that no commas are necessary between the state and the ZIP code.

However, when alluding to a city and state in a sentence (without the ZIP code), use a comma after the state.

Example:

I traveled through St. Louis, MO, on my way to Chicago.

The same rule applies for a city and country as well:

> Sometimes Elaine travels to Paris, France, in the fall.

Salutations and Closings

When writing a letter, use a comma after the person's name and after your closing. Note that a business letter salutation requires a colon rather than a comma.

	PERSONAL LETTER	BUSINESS LETTER
Salutation	Dear Aunt Rosie,	Dear Sir/Madam:
Closing	Love,	Sincerely,
	Yours truly,	Respectfully,
	Fondly,	Best regards,

Rule 5. Use commas before the coordinating conjunction *for, and, nor, but, or, yet,* or *so* if it is followed by an independent clause.

Examples:

Frank is retired**, and** his wife, Louise, will retire this year.

Frank is retired**, yet** his wife, Louise, will work for another three years.

Rule 6. Use commas before, within, and after direct quotations (the exact words someone says), whether the speaker is identified at the beginning or the end.

Examples:

Drew said**,** "Our trip to Aruba was awesome."

"Our trip to Aruba**,**" Drew said**,** "was awesome."

"Our trip to Aruba was awesome**,**" Drew said.

Note that an indirect quote means someone is conveying what someone else said. Do not use commas to set off the speaker in an indirect quotation.

Example:

Drew said that their trip to Aruba was awesome.

Rule 7. Commas are used with titles and degrees only when they follow the person's name.

Examples:

Arthur Mari**,** M.D.

Sandy Dugan**,** Ph.D.

Dr. Foster

Dr. Sandy Dugan

Rule 8. Commas are used when writing numbers longer than three digits.

In order to make a long number like 1479363072 easier to read, it is customary to place commas by grouping numbers into threes from **right to left**, dividing them into thousands, ten-thousands, hundred-thousands, and so on: 1,479,363,072.

Exceptions to this rule are phone numbers, page numbers, ZIP codes, years, serial numbers, and house numbers.

Example:

Edison, NJ, has five ZIP codes: 08817, 08818, 08820, 08837, and 08899.

As in any other series, commas should be placed between whole **numbers in a series of numbers.**

Example:

Refer to pages 466**,** 467**,** and 468 in the phone book to find information on ZIP codes.

TIP

Read each sentence you write aloud to see where you would naturally pause to take a breath before the end. That is where you may need to put a comma.

Practice

Add commas where necessary in the following sentences or phrases.

1. His list of things to buy at the store included apples butter wheat bread and orange juice.

2. Because the chorus member had laryngitis she couldn't sing in the show on Tuesday Wednesday or Thursday.

3. "Oh I didn't know you were here" she said "or I wouldn't have played the music so loud."

4. Houston Texas is the site of the annual Chili Festival where they feature amateur cooks local restaurants and great chili recipes from all over the country.

5. Either I'm going crazy or some kind of animal is making noise in the attic.

6. She had to buy the dog a new bed for he had chewed up his old one.

7. The nurse disinfected the cut on my hand put a bandage on it and told me to be more careful when slicing bagels.

8. When I ran into my favorite celebrity on the street in New York she graciously agreed to have a picture taken with me Aunt Sally and my dad.

9. For our anniversary in September which will be our third we will be vacationing in Acapulco Mexico.

10. The twins actually have different birthdays because Nicholas was born at 11:58 P.M. on Monday June 3 and Nathan was born at 12:02 A.M. on Tuesday June 4.

Colons

Colons are used to introduce a word, sentence, list, quotation, or phrase. They say "here is an example" or "an example is going to follow."

Example:
On your first day of the art workshop, please bring the following items to room 601 of Larsson Hall: a charcoal pencil, two paintbrushes, a drawing pad, and your creativity.

Do not use a colon when introducing a list if the colon follows a preposition or a verb.

Incorrect:
On your first day of the art workshop, please bring: a charcoal pencil, two paintbrushes, a drawing pad, and your creativity to room 601 of Larsson Hall.

A colon can also introduce an excerpt or long quotation in your writing.

Example:
Benjamin Franklin (1706–1790), diplomat, politician, physicist, writer, and inventor, is quoted as saying: "All human situations have their inconveniences. We feel those of the present but neither see nor feel those of the future; and hence we often make troublesome changes without amendment, and frequently for the worse."

A colon can set off the subtitle of a movie or book.

Examples:
Phenomenal Women: Four Poems Celebrating Women is written by Maya Angelou, one of America's finest female poets.
Jimmy has watched *Barnyard: The Original Party* four times this weekend.

Colons are used to separate the hour from minutes in written time.

The next bus for New York City leaves at 10:20 A.M.

A colon is also used between numbers when citing the volume and pages of books and magazines.

Please refer to Volume 3: pages 4–9 for further information.

Semicolons

Also called the "super comma," the **semicolon** is used to link two topic-related independent clauses (sentences) when a coordinating conjunction is not used.

Examples:

Steven's sister, Haley, is short. Steven is tall.

Steven's sister, Haley, is short; Steven is tall.

Do not join the two clauses with a comma instead of a semicolon, as doing so would create what is called a comma splice.

Use a semicolon between two independent clauses joined by a coordinating conjunction (*for, and, nor, but, or, yet,* or *so*) only when commas are also used in the sentence.

Example:

Because Haley is 6′2″ tall, she is taller than most people; *but* she is the shortest sibling in her family.

Use a semicolon between two independent clauses separated by a transitional word or phrase or by a conjunctive adverb.

Example:

At 6′8″, Steven is tall; *therefore,* even at 6′2″, Steven's sister, Haley, is short in her family.

COMMON CONJUNCTIVE ADVERBS		
afterward	accordingly	besides
coincidentally	consequently	furthermore
hence	however	indeed
instead	likewise	moreover
nevertheless	nonetheless	otherwise
similarly	so	still
then	therefore	thus

Practice

Add colons and semicolons where necessary in the following sentences.

11. On his to-do list, he had the following items rake the yard, call the plumber, pick up Chinese takeout for dinner, and call Francine.

12. His new book, *The CEO Secret Finding Your Inner Executive,* is available for sale now if you go to the bookstore on Saturday, he'll be signing copies.

13. The Tampa Bay Rays have lost six games in a row however, I believe they can still turn things around and make the playoffs.

14. The book had the following dedication "To Rosemary I couldn't have done this without you."

15. After the scandal broke, the disgraced celebrity made a statement to the press "No comment."

16. Peggy knew she would have to tell the truth to Pete eventually she hoped he'd forget about the topic in the meantime, though.

17. After counting all of my money, I discovered that I had $1,453 in my savings account $756 in my checking account and $43 in my change jar, which I keep on my dresser.

18. At 400, Roger realized that Chantelle probably wasn't coming he waited for ten more minutes just in case, then went home.

19. Jamie wants to borrow these DVDs from you *Gray's Anatomy*, seasons 1 and 2 *Law & Order*, season 3 and *The Vampire Diaries*, season 1.

20. Our power went out during the hurricane three days later, we're still waiting for the power company to fix it.

Answers

1. His list of things to buy at the store included apples, butter, wheat bread, and orange juice.

2. Because the chorus member had laryngitis, she couldn't sing in the show on Tuesday, Wednesday, or Thursday.

3. "Oh, I didn't know you were here," she said, "or I wouldn't have played the music so loud."

4. Houston, Texas, is the site of the annual Chili Festival, where they feature amateur cooks, local restaurants, and great chili recipes from all over the country.

5. Either I'm going crazy or some kind of animal is making noise in the attic.

6. She had to buy the dog a new bed, for he had chewed up his old one.

7. The nurse disinfected the cut on my hand, put a bandage on it, and told me to be more careful when slicing bagels.

8. When I ran into my favorite celebrity on the street in New York, she graciously agreed to have a picture taken with me, Aunt Sally, and my dad.

9. For our anniversary in September, which will be our third, we will be vacationing in Acapulco, Mexico.

10. The twins actually have different birthdays, because Nicholas was born at 11:58 P.M. on Monday, June 3, and Nathan was born at 12:02 A.M. on Tuesday, June 4.

11. On his to-do list, he had the following items: rake the yard, call the plumber, pick up Chinese takeout for dinner, and call Francine.

12. His new book, *The CEO Secret: Finding Your Inner Executive*, is available for sale now; if you go to the bookstore on Saturday, he'll be signing copies.

13. The Tampa Bay Rays have lost six games in a row; however, I believe they can still turn things around and make the playoffs.

14. The book had the following dedication: "To Rosemary: I couldn't have done this without you."

15. After the scandal broke, the disgraced celebrity made a statement to the press: "No comment."

16. Peggy knew she would have to tell the truth to Pete eventually; she hoped he'd forget about the topic in the meantime, though.

17. After counting all of my money, I discovered that I had $1,453 in my savings account; $756 in my checking account; and $43 in my change jar, which I keep on my dresser.

18. At 4:00, Roger realized that Chantelle probably wasn't coming; he waited for ten more minutes just in case, then went home.

19. Jamie wants to borrow these DVDs from you: *Gray's Anatomy*, seasons 1 and 2; *Law & Order*, season 3; and *The Vampire Diaries*, season 1.

20. Our power went out during the hurricane; three days later, we're still waiting for the power company to fix it.

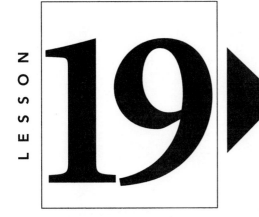

19 ▶ INTERNAL PUNCTUATION II

But through every clause and part of speech of the right book I meet the eyes of the most determined men; his force and terror inundate every word: the commas and dashes are alive; so that the writing is athletic and nimble,—can go far and live long.

—Ralph Waldo Emerson, American essayist,
poet, and philosopher (1803–1882)

LESSON SUMMARY

Knowing when and how to use contractions or show *possession*, and whether to *divide*, *join*, *interrupt*, or *emphasize* your words and phrases correctly, is essential in good writing. This lesson shows you when and how.

Apostrophes

Apostrophes are used to create contractions, to make nouns possessive, and, in rare instances, to make a noun plural.

Contractions

Contract (con-TRACT) means to squeeze together or shorten. In informal writing, we shorten two words into one, using an apostrophe to create a **contraction**. For instance, *has* and *not* would become *hasn't*. The following tables show some other common contractions.

PRONOUN CONTRACTIONS				
	AM/IS/ARE	WILL	HAVE/HAS	HAD/WOULD
I	I'm	I'll	I've	I'd
you	you're	you'll	you've	you'd
he	he's	he'll	he's	he'd
she	she's	she'll	she's	she'd
it	it's	it'll	it's	it'd
we	we're	we'll	we've	we'd
they	they're	they'll	they've	they'd

HELPING VERB CONTRACTIONS				
is	+	not	=	isn't
are	+	not	=	aren't
was	+	not	=	wasn't
were	+	not	=	weren't
have	+	not	=	haven't
has	+	not	=	hasn't
had	+	not	=	hadn't
might	+	not	=	mightn't
can	+	not	=	can't
do	+	not	=	don't
did	+	not	=	didn't
should	+	not	=	shouldn't
would	+	not	=	wouldn't
could	+	not	=	couldn't

Note that contractions are not used in formal writing. Use formal writing mainly for academic or business communications; use informal, or more casual, writing for reader-friendly messages.

Possessive Nouns

Possessives are nouns that show ownership. To make a singular noun possessive, add -'s. Be careful not to confuse the plural form of a noun with the possessive.

Plural Form:
The writer of the news **stories** won a Pulitzer.

Singular Possessive:
The news **story's** writer won a Pulitzer.

The first sentence tells us that the writer of multiple stories won a Pulitzer. The second sentence tells us the writer of one story won a Pulitzer.

To form the possessive of the plural noun *stories*, add an apostrophe after the final -s.

Plural Possessive:
The news **stories'** writer won a Pulitzer.

This sentence also tells us that the writer of multiple stories won a Pulitzer. The -s' rule applies only to plural nouns ending with an -s. For example, the possessive of the plural noun *children* would be *children's*.

To form the possessive of a singular noun ending with -s, add -'s. However, certain proper names such as *Jesus* and *Socrates* are exceptions to this rule.

Examples:
I finally met my **boss's** wife.
Jesus' portrait hangs over my fireplace.

Plurals with Apostrophe + s

There are a few occasions when -'s is required to make a noun plural.

Add -'s to form the plural of abbreviations that contain more than one period, such as Ph.D. or M.D.

Example:
M.D.'s and **Ph.D.'s** are doctorate degrees in medicine and philosophy.

Add -'s to form the plural of words, letters, and numbers that we do not commonly see in the plural form.

Examples:
How many **um's** and **uh's** did you count in the run-through of my speech?
I got four **A's** and two **B's** on my report card.
Please write your **5's** and **8's** more clearly on tests.

Practice

Place apostrophes where they belong in the following sentences.

1. Grannys recipe for apple pie was featured in *Ladies Home Journal* in 1964.

2. Jesss bike was stolen after she forgot to lock it outside the library.

3. Paul and Joanies house has been on the market for six months now.

4. "Its a shame you couldnt make it to Jennys party," Orville said.

5. Remember, when you set out the cats food: Mr. Sniffles gets the special food for elderly cats, and Buddy gets the regular kibble.

6. The classes test results put them among the top scorers in the state.

7. Why dont you set that box down over there, next to Louiss suitcase?

8. I borrowed Melanies and Jasons notes, because I missed Mondays class.

9. Your entry wont count if you dont make sure its postmarked by the contests deadline of January 15.

10. Youre the expert here, so I could use your advice.

Hyphens and Dashes

Although they look similar, hyphens and dashes perform completely different jobs: hyphens and en-dashes divide and join, whereas em-dashes interrupt and emphasize. Knowing the difference will help you better identify them in your reading and correctly utilize them in your writing.

Hyphens

Hyphens divide words at the ends of lines, separate numbers, join compound words, and attach prefixes and suffixes.

To divide a word at the end of a line of typed text, place a hyphen at a syllable break in the word.

Examples:
cir-cum-stance
ab-bre-vi-a-tion
poly-vi-nyl

TIP

Syllables are the individual spoken units of a word, consisting of a vowel or a vowel-consonant combination. To find syllable breaks in a word, simply tap your finger or clap your hand for each spoken unit. The word syllable, for instance, has three separate audible units: syl, la, and ble. To write the syllables, divide the correctly spelled word into the units you hear. (Note that not all dictionaries agree on the breakdown of all word units.)

Hyphens are used to join many prefixes, such as *great-*, *all-*, *half-*, *ex-*, and *self-*, and the suffix *-elect*, to existing words in order to create a new word:

great-grandfather	great-aunt
all-encompassing	all-American
half-moon	half-life
ex-wife	ex-mayor
self-esteem	self-regulated
governor-elect	president-elect

Hyphens are also used to turn phrases into a single unit:

sister-in-law jack-in-the-box forget-me-not

They are used to separate word units when spelling out the numbers 21 to 99 or fractions,

thirty-six ninety-nine six-eighths one-fourth

and in dates:

The article from the 08-23-06 *Chicago Sun* edition was incorrect.

Hyphens are useful to avoid confusion.

Example:
Mr. Johnson tried to recollect how he planned to **re-collect** the student's papers this time to avoid unnecessary chaos.

They are also helpful when spelling certain compound words that would look awkward otherwise.

Example:
The button's **shell-like** appearance made it intriguing.

Without the hyphen, *shell-like* would become *shelllike*, with three *l*'s crashing together!

Remember, not all prefixes require a hyphen. Usually, a hyphen is used when a letter becomes doubled or tripled, or if the added prefix creates a spelling similar to that of another word. Always check a dictionary if you are not sure.

En-Dashes

En-dashes can replace *to* in scores.

The Red Sox beat the White Sox 10–3 on Friday.

Em-Dashes

Em-dashes are used to indicate incidental thoughts in writing.

Example:
Louis's favorite color is—let me guess—pink!

Like a colon, but less formal, an em-dash can be used to set off a short series of phrases or words in a sentence.

Example:
I bought what I needed—lipstick, blush, eye shadow, liner pencils, and foundation—at the department store cosmetics counter.

TIP

When using em-dashes, make sure that the parts of the sentence before and after them would make sense if you were to remove the em-dashes and the words they set off.

Practice

Determine where hyphens or em-dashes should be appropriately placed in the following sentences.

11. I'm really lucky I get along well with my mother in law and father in law.

12. Everyone was curious about what the president elect would say in his election night victory speech.

13. This is my favorite T shirt I've worn it so much that you can barely tell what color it was originally.

14. Minnie thought the other player was bluffing, so she went all in on her poker hand.

15. It wasn't until the mid 1980s that the band became popular but since then, they've been a constant presence.

16. We won't know the test scores until tomorrow at that point, we can figure out if we need to retake the test.

17. Marcy never one to shy away from conflict confronted the man who had cut in front of her in the checkout line.

18. Shani went to the all American team's rally, but left after the first few speeches.

19. His favorite historical period to study is pre Columbian America but World War II is a close second.

20. More often than not, his devil may care attitude got him in trouble.

Answers

1. Granny's recipe for apple pie was featured in *Ladies' Home Journal* in 1964.

2. Jess's bike was stolen after she forgot to lock it outside the library.

3. Paul and Joanie's house has been on the market for six months now.

4. "It's a shame you couldn't make it to Jenny's party," Orville said.

5. Remember, when you set out the cats' food: Mr. Sniffles gets the special food for elderly cats, and Buddy gets the regular kibble.

6. The classes' test results put them among the top scorers in the state.

7. Why don't you set that box down over there, next to Louis's suitcase?

8. I borrowed Melanie's and Jason's notes, because I missed Monday's class.

9. Your entry won't count if you don't make sure it's postmarked by the contest's deadline of January 15.

10. You're the expert here, so I could use your advice.

11. I'm really lucky—I get along well with my mother-in-law and father-in-law.

12. Everyone was curious about what the president-elect would say in his election night victory speech.

13. This is my favorite T-shirt—I've worn it so much that you can barely tell what color it was originally.

14. Minnie thought the other player was bluffing, so she went all-in on her poker hand.

15. It wasn't until the mid-1980s that the band became popular—but since then, they've been a constant presence.

16. We won't know the test scores until tomorrow—at that point, we can figure out if we need to retake the test.

17. Marcy—never one to shy away from conflict—confronted the man who had cut in front of her in the checkout line.

18. Shani went to the all-American team's rally, but left after the first few speeches.

19. His favorite historical period to study is pre-Columbian America—but World War II is a close second.

20. More often than not, his devil-may-care attitude got him in trouble.

20 ▶ INTERNAL PUNCTUATION III

It is an old error of man to forget to put quotation marks where he borrows from a woman's brain!

—Anna Garlin Spencer, American educator, author, and feminist (1851–1931)

LESSON SUMMARY

It is helpful to know how to write dialogue, insert a parenthetical comment, and editorialize in your writing. Learn the proper way to do these things in this lesson.

Quotation Marks

Quotation marks are used in writing to show someone's exact words, or dialogue. This word-for-word account is called a **direct quotation**. To set the direct quotation apart, you need to use opening and ending quotation marks: " and ".

If someone just *refers* to someone else's words, this is called an **indirect quotation**, which does NOT require quotation marks.

Example:

Margaret said that the teller patiently told her to please enter the code again.

Quotation marks also are not used in recording someone's thoughts.

Example:

Margaret thought the teller had a lot of patience.

We sometimes put quotation marks around a word (or words) to stress its meaning or to convey uncertainty or misgivings about its validity to readers.

Example:

It escapes me why Victor, a Wall Street broker, was asked to speak to our Lifeguard Association as an "expert" on rescue techniques.

Practice

Place quotation marks, commas, and end marks in the following sentences, and change to caps as needed, or note that they are correct as written.

1. "oh my goodness" she exclaimed, startled by the unexpected fireworks.

2. When Bobby brewer the superstar player struck out for the third time in a row the stadium erupted in angry shouts of booooo

3. The label on the paint can said the color was pacific turquoise but it looked more like regular green to me

4. "Can you put this away for me" she asked tossing me the box of crackers

5. "Bad dog" Evelyn yelled, while grover a yorkshire terrier, lowered his head and slunk away from the damaged couch.

6. This is the best french toast I've ever eaten

7. Our boat the *mademoiselle Marie* was put away for the winter at dockside marina.

8. Argus's report card said that he was "too disruptive" in class, and should pay more attention during lessons.

9. Wow thanks he yelled joyfully after finding his new bike parked in front of the Christmas tree.

10. Which house is the Jorgenson family's

Parentheses

Parentheses are used to provide extra or incidental information within or at the end of a sentence. The information inside the parentheses is called a **parenthetical comment**.

Example:
Ron Kenny wound up with the Salesperson of the Year Award (remember how he struggled at the beginning of the year?).

Note that even if you take the parenthetical comment out of the sentence, it still makes sense.

Parentheses also set off dates and page numbers within sentences or in citations in some styles of academic writing.

Examples:
Information regarding the migration of Monarch butterflies can be found in Chapter 22 (pages 97–113).
In a famous study of Jane Austen (1775–1817) and her many literary accomplishments (Dawson, 1989) . . .

Parentheses can be used for itemizing numbers or letters:

Please write your (1) name, (2) address, and (3) DOB.
Please write your (a) name, (b) address, and (c) DOB.

TIP

If your parenthetical comment is part of the whole sentence, do not put a period or other end mark inside the parentheses. But if the note is a complete sentence, put a punctuation mark inside the parentheses.

Parentheses are also used for providing, or defining, abbreviations.

Examples:

There has been recent news from the National Aeronautics and Space Administration (NASA) . . .

The Federal Communications Commission (FCC) has issued a new . . .

Finally, parentheses can be used to indicate an alternative form of a written term.

Examples:

Before printing, carefully select the page(s) you need.

Write the name(s) on the form and submit.

Practice

Determine where parentheses should be placed in the following sentences.

11. Bob Flenderson a famous anthropologist returned from his work in the Amazon rain forest last week.

12. Anya moved to the United States when she was 17 which was in 1996.

13. The Florida Gators' record 16–2 is the best in their conference.

14. Did you know that the escalator is out of order and has been for more than a week?

15. Those doughnuts are amazing I ate at least three of them.

Brackets

Brackets also help to clarify information, but they have a narrower range of uses than parentheses.

When you editorialize (insert comments or missing material within a quote), place the words inside brackets.

Example:

Kim said, "In order for you [Katelyn] to go [to the Monmouth Mall to see a movie], you must finish the dishes first."

If the capitalization of a word in a quote needs to be altered in order to make it fit in a sentence or paragraph scheme, place the new letter in brackets.

Example:

The *New York Times* article stated that "[b]aseball, an American pastime, is favored by many women as well as children."

Note that the article would have read *"Baseball, an American pastime . . ."* in the original source.

Practice

Determine where brackets belong in the following sentences.

16. According to the article, "The student Julia Marquez won the prestigious Crawford Scholarship to study at Burnley Music Academy."

17. He moved to Boston to start an internship at Marley Stearns (a prestigious though unpaid position).

18. The magazine article on Joe's disappearance featured an interview with his wife: "I have no idea where Joe went. If you find him, let me know."

19. The study reported that "the relationship between them the drug and potential side effects is unclear."

20. She pronounced the trip "an unmitigated disaster."

Italics and Underlining

When writing by hand, italicizing words is difficult, so we underline them instead. In printing and word processing, we can use either one (although underscores are uncommon). Just remember to be consistent. Don't use one and then another for the same purpose in the same text.

Italicize (or underline) the titles of long works such as books, long poems, magazines, newspapers, or movies.

Examples:

James Michener's   James Michener's
  Chesapeake   Chesapeake
The New Yorker   The New Yorker
Robert Frost's *Birches*   Robert Frost's Birches

Set off shorter works such as stories, songs, short poems, and articles with quotation marks rather than italics or underlines.

Italicize foreign words in your writing.

Example:
The handsome man said, "*Ciao bella*," when he left the table.

When you want to emphasize a particular word, italicize (or underline) it. The following chart shows how emphasizing different words in a sentence can change the meaning completely.

SAME SENTENCE, FOUR DIFFERENT MEANINGS	
I like your shoes.	It is I, and only I, who likes them
I *like* your shoes.	Don't love them, just like them
I like *your* shoes.	No one else's but yours
I like your *shoes*.	Not your outfit or your hair, but your shoes

Practice

Identify the words and phrases that need to be italicized (or underlined) in the following sentences.

21. We finally got tickets to see Cat on a Hot Tin Roof on Broadway.

22. Our cruise ship was called the Jewel of the Seven Seas.

23. The Daily Show, 60 Minutes, and the Today show are my favorite current-events TV shows.

24. The keys for the letters a, q, and p are sticking on my keyboard.

25. He has a certain je ne sais quois that draws me to him.

Answers

1. "Oh, my goodness!" she exclaimed, startled by the unexpected fireworks.

2. When Bobby Brewer, the superstar player, struck out for the third time in a row, the stadium erupted in angry shouts of "Booooo!"

3. The label on the paint can said the color was "Pacific Turquoise," but it looked more like regular green to me.

4. "Can you put this away for me?" she asked, tossing me the box of crackers.

5. "Bad dog!" Evelyn yelled, while Grover, a Yorkshire terrier, lowered his head and slunk away from the damaged couch.

6. This is the best French toast I've ever eaten!

7. Our boat, the *Mademoiselle Marie*, was put away for the winter at Dockside Marina.

8. This sentence is correct as is.

9. "Wow, thanks!" he yelled joyfully after finding his new bike parked in front of the Christmas tree.

10. Which house is the Jorgenson family's?

11. Bob Flenderson (a famous anthropologist) returned from his work in the Amazon rain forest last week.

12. Anya moved to the United States when she was 17 (which was in 1996).

13. The Florida Gators' record (16–2) is the best in their conference.

14. Did you know that the escalator is out of order (and has been for more than a week)?

15. Those doughnuts are amazing (I ate at least three of them).

16. According to the article, "The student [Julia Marquez] won the prestigious Crawford Scholarship to study at Burnley Music Academy."

17. He moved to Boston to start an internship at Marley Stearns (a prestigious [though unpaid] position).

18. The magazine article on Joe's disappearance featured an interview with his wife: "I have no idea [where Joe went]. If you find him, let me know."

19. The study reported that "the relationship between them [the drug and potential side effects] is unclear."

20. She pronounced the trip "[a]n unmitigated disaster."

21. *Cat on a Hot Tin Roof*

22. *Jewel of the Seven Seas*

23. *The Daily Show*, *60 Minutes*, and the *Today* show

24. *a*, *q*, and *p*

25. *je ne sais quois*

POSTTEST

Now that you have spent a good deal of time improving your grammar skills, take this posttest to see how much you have learned. Record your answers in this book. If it does not belong to you, list the numbers 1–50 on a piece of paper and write your answers there. Take as much time as you need to finish the test. When you do, check your answers against the correct answers in the section that follows. Each answer lists the lesson of the book that covers the concept(s) in that question.

If you took the pretest at the beginning of the book, you can compare what you knew then with what you know now. Check your score on this posttest against your score on the pretest. If this score is much higher, congratulations—you have profited noticeably from your hard work. If your score shows little improvement, you may want to review certain chapters, especially if you see a pattern to the kinds of questions you missed. Whatever your score, keep this book handy for review and reference whenever you are unsure of a grammatical rule.

Posttest

1. Circle the common nouns.

pillow	jealousy	fruit
guilt	kindness	breathe
information	clapping	mindless
FBI	cute	razor

2. Circle the abstract nouns.

knowledge	log	pleasure
deceit	pilot	jury
malice	money	banana split
carrots	warmth	hope

3. Circle the proper nouns.

Violin	Chair	President Obama
Harvard	Sabrina	Memphis
Lunch	Earth	Idaho
NBC	Lamps	Pacific

4. Circle the nouns that are pluralized correctly.

televisions	flys	mouses
womans	tooths	analyses
ferries	deers	igloos
knifes	pluses	volcanoes

5. Circle the hyphenated nouns that are spelled correctly.

| frees-for-all | not-for-profits |
| fathers-in-law | voice-overs |

6. Circle the nouns that have been made possessive correctly.

horse's	ants's	doctors'
kittens's	bus'	teachers'
children's	classes'	Max's
bands's	child's	class's

7. Circle the antecedents/pronouns that properly agree in gender.

Matt/her	lizard/it
mice/they	Cheryl/she
students/it	you and I/we

8. Circle the antecedents/pronouns that properly agree in number.

kites/they	everyone/they	Paul and I/we
fishermen/they	company/it	deer/it
each/we	player/we	deer/they

9. Circle the interrogative pronouns.

where	when	who
whom	whoever	whose
how	which	whatever

10. Circle the subjective case pronouns.

They gave me the Miss Congeniality award!

She never seems to have time to visit her old neighborhood.

We picked a lot of peaches from our trees.

11. Circle the objective case pronouns.

We lent it to him.

Give me a sign.

He cooked them ravioli.

12. Circle the reflexive case pronouns and underline the possessive case pronouns.

Andrew questioned himself about his decision to buy the treadmill.

His decision about buying the treadmill was rash.

Heather herself wondered what prompted him to buy it.

13. Circle the demonstrative pronouns and underline the relative pronouns.

This isn't a good way to spend the money that you saved!

Is that the neighbor who drove you home from the airport?

14. Circle the action verbs.

look	talk	help	cook
just	draw	itch	be
moisten	should	may	geranium

15. Circle the helping and linking verbs.

take	can	now	not
never	will	are	could
would	am	how	did

16. Circle the regular verbs and underline the irregular verbs.

injure	lock	carry	write
untie	hide	mow	drive
know	grow	cost	throw

17. Circle the correct form of lay/lie in each sentence.

Sammy usually (lays, lies) his schoolbooks on his desk.

This mysterious trunk has (lain, laid) untouched in this attic for decades.

The shopkeeper (laid, lain) his apron on the counter before locking up for the night.

18. Circle the correct form of sit/set in each sentence.

Janice is (setting, sitting) the table before her guests arrive.

Jim (sat, set) down in the comfortable chair and took a short nap.

We had (set, sat) our glasses of lemonade on the orange coasters beside us.

19. Circle the correct tricky words in each sentence.

"Mom, (can, may) I sell some of this old jewelry online?" I asked.

He answered every question on the exam correctly (accept, except) the last one.

Marcy, Chris, and I (hanged, hung) out at the mall almost all day Saturday.

20. Identify the tense of the verbs that follow as present, past, future, present perfect, past perfect, future perfect, present progressive, past progressive, or future progressive.

am swimming	had swum
will have swum	swam
have swum	will swim
were swimming	swims

21. Circle the common adjectives in the following sentences.

Sanjay lent his laptop computer to his long-time friend Benjamin.

Soccer is the most popular sport in the world; however, Nathan prefers tennis.

Elvis was a legendary rock-and-roll performer who was loved by people everywhere.

22. Place the correct indefinite article in front of each noun.

___ hen	___ hour-long lecture
___ honorable person	___ universe
___ one-car family	___ wristwatch
___ orthodontist	___ upperclassman
___ honeybee	___ elegant dinner
___ orangutan	___ underwater city
___ ozone layer	___ opinion
___ umbrella	

23. Circle the proper adjectives.

Samoan	patrician	Irish
Canadian	Paris	Washingtonian
Antarctic	Milwaukee	spartan

24. Determine whether the boldfaced word in each sentence is a possessive pronoun or a possessive adjective.

I showed Charles **my** coin collection, and he told me about **his**.

Her kindness was undeniable; she would always share what was **hers** with others.

Our hunch was that the deed was really **theirs**, but only time would tell.

25. Determine whether the boldfaced word in each sentence is a demonstrative pronoun or a demonstrative adjective.

That storm isn't moving fast enough to suit me.

Hand me **those**, please, before you drop them.

This has got to be the fastest time you've recorded yet.

26. Determine which form of comparative or superlative adjective best completes each sentence.

The (cooler, coolest) day yet this week was Wednesday, and it was 97 degrees.

Yuck! This rock is (slimy, slimier) than the other one.

My shoes are the (narrower, narrowest) of all.

27. Circle the correct form of the comparative and superlative adverbs in the following sentences.

Of the three jockeys, Marco rode (more cautiously, most cautiously) during the race.

My flight from L.A. to Tucson seemed (longer, longest) than the one from Tucson to New York.

People said my coconut custard pie tasted good; in fact, Sam said it tasted (better, best) than his mom's!

28. Determine whether the boldfaced word in the sentence is an adjective or an adverb.

Lori told Joe not to be too **hard** on himself.

Living in **close** quarters can be difficult for some.

Kyle went **straight** home after the movie.

29. Identify the prepositional phrases in the following sentences.

Termites were found all around the building.

Without a word, he finished dinner and went upstairs to his room.

We drove around the back to drop off the heaviest packages first.

30. Determine whether the boldfaced word is a preposition or an adverb.

If you spin **around** quickly, you'll probably get dizzy.

We went **out** for ice cream when the show was over.

She walked quickly **across** the room to see what had crashed to the floor.

31. Rewrite each sentence so that the misplaced modifiers are properly placed.

Having been burned to a crisp, the chef threw the roast into the sink.

Crocks of onion soup were served to the guests dripping with cheese.

At the age of five, Kerry's parents brought her to Walt Disney World.

32. Using the clues, write the homonyms, homophones, or homographs.

    group of cattle/listened

    give a lecture/where you live

    stumble/an excursion

    passed away/changed the color

    fair-minded/barely

    shoreline/glide without power

    authentic/spool of film

    behavior/run [e.g., an experiment]

33. Identify the simple subject in the following sentences.

    Animals that sleep during the day and are awake at night are called nocturnal.

    Artificial intelligence is used not only in games, but for medical purposes as well.

    Please stop.

    Most liked it, although some did not.

    Although he lives on his own, Mike still likes coming home once in a while.

34. Identify the simple predicate in the following sentences.

    Jane played hopscotch all afternoon.

    Stand still, please.

    We spotted a turtle on a rock nearby.

35. Identify whether the boldfaced word is a direct or an indirect object in the following sentences.

    The orchestra played several Beethoven **pieces**.

    The townspeople gave the **sheriff** a welcoming **ovation**.

    The judge gave the contest **finalists** extra **time** to prepare for the last round.

36. Identify the predicate nouns and predicate adjectives in the following sentences.

    On the hot summer day, Jay's turkey and mayo sandwich turned bad.

    Cockatiels can become speaking birds if trained well.

    Judy was a pie chef who entered and won many contests.

37. Identify the verb that correctly completes the following sentences.

    Bacon and eggs (are, is) the favorite dish of many people who stop at our diner.

    Kara and Maria (try, tries) out for the community theater's musical production every year.

    Science fiction or mystery (are, is) the only choice of genre left to choose from for my report.

38. Identify the verb that will agree with the indefinite pronouns in the following sentences.

    Everyone (go, goes) to the prom each year.

    Something (need, needs) to be done about that leak.

    While each (prefers, prefer) to eat yogurt, the time of day it's eaten varies widely.

39. Determine which pronoun best fits for proper pronoun-antecedent agreement in each sentence.

    The group took _____ yearly retreat to Maine.

    Everyone carefully opened _____ package.

    The puppy wagged _____ tail eagerly when it saw the mailman at the door.

40. Identify the adjective and adverb phrases in the following sentences.

Some of the shoes on the far shelf cost more than $300.

The airline representative said the flight should arrive within the hour.

Even though I hung the picture up carefully, it still fell from the wall.

41. Identify the participial phrases, infinitive phrases, and gerund phrases in the following sentences.

Becoming an accomplished pianist has always been Victoria's plan.

To avoid slipping on the ice, wear boots or shoes with a ridged sole.

Leaving his entire fortune to his nephew Lewis, Zach signed his will with little trepidation.

42. Identify the appositive phrases in the following sentences.

I received a great letter of recommendation for a summer internship from Professor Williams, the head of our science department.

Billie Jean King, a professional tennis player, was the first female athlete to win over $100,000 in prize money in a single season.

The American holly has been the state tree of Delaware, the first state to ratify the U.S. Constitution, since 1939.

43. Determine whether each group of words is an independent or a subordinate clause.

as I said

I am learning ballroom dancing

here are some for you

well, I should say so

that's life

stop that

44. Identify the adjective clause in each sentence.

I sang a song that my mom sang to me when I was a baby.

The boy who is at the end of the line closed the door.

The Asian market where they sell many exotic fruits is down the road from us.

45. Identify the noun clause in each sentence.

I know that drinking water is better than drinking soda.

Do you know what time the store opens?

I can't decide which shoes to wear.

46. Identify the adverb clause in each sentence.

Except for Tanya, we all got soaked while we walked back from the auditorium.

Whether or not you believe it, the decision is ultimately yours.

Violet decided to go home for the holidays since her grandparents would be visiting, too.

47. Identify the coordinating conjunction in each sentence and the words or groups of words it is connecting.

Gold or blue would be the best choice of color for the pillows.

Danielle and Joanna watched a movie, popped popcorn, and stayed up all night talking.

Sometimes we go to the lake so we can water-ski.

48. Identify the simple, compound, complex, and compound-complex sentences.

    a. Some citizens voted in the town election, but many did not.

    b. If you want to make mashed potatoes, just add butter and milk to the boiled potatoes and mash until creamy.

    c. Put your folded laundry away, please.

    d. Because Jill was late, she missed the introductory overview of the entire workshop.

49. Add punctuation where necessary in the following sentences.

    On April 12 1861 the Civil War began with the battle at Fort Sumter

    The dentists hygienists and staff threw a surprise party for him

    Would you consider using Benjis or Jesss racket for now

50. Correctly place quotation marks, commas, and end marks in the following sentences.

    It's not easy to memorize all of the mathematical formulas for algebra stated Mrs. Shapiro but we'll accomplish that by the year's end

    Would you make my steak sandwich without onions please asked Harry

    I began Courtney am not the only girl who feels that way

Answers

If you miss any of the following questions, you may refer to the designated lesson for further explanation.

1. The common nouns are *pillow*, *fruit*, *information*, and *razor*. These are all general terms, and are not associated with proper names. Of the other options, *jealousy*, *guilt*, and *kindness* are concepts or ideas, so they are abstract nouns; *breathe* and *clapping* are verbs; and *mindless* and *cute* are adjectives. (Lesson 1)

2. The abstract nouns are *knowledge*, *pleasure*, *deceit*, *malice*, and *hope*. Abstract nouns express a concept or idea. Of the other options, *log*, *pilot*, *jury*, *money*, *banana split*, *carrots*, and *warmth* are all common nouns. (Lesson 1)

3. The proper nouns are *President Obama*, *Harvard*, *Sabrina*, *Memphis*, *Earth*, *Idaho*, *NBC*, and *Pacific*. All are names of specific people, places, or companies. (Lesson 1)

4. The correct answers are *televisions*, *analyses*, *ferries*, *igloos*, *pluses*, and *volcanoes*. Of the other options, *flys* should change the *-ys* to *-ies*. *Mouse*, *woman*, *tooth*, and *deer* are all irregular nouns, with the plurals *mice*, *women*, *teeth*, and *deer*. And finally, remember that *-ife* words like *knife* become plural with the ending *-ives*. (Lesson 2)

5. The correct answers are *not-for-profits*, *fathers-in-law*, and *voice-overs*. These hyphenated compound nouns add the *-s* to the word that changes in number. *Frees-for-all* incorrectly pluralizes the adjective, not the count noun. (Lesson 2)

6. The correct answers are *horse's*, *doctors'*, *teachers'*, *children's*, *classes'*, *Max's*, *child's*, and *class's*. (Lesson 2)

7. The correct answers are:

lizard/it

mice/they

Cheryl/she

you and I/we

Lizard is singular and an animal, so it takes the neutral, singular pronoun *it. Mice* and *you and I* are both plural, so they take the plural pronouns *they* and *we. Cheryl* is a female name, so *she* is the correct pronoun. *Students* is plural, so the singular pronoun *it* is incorrect. The name *Matt* is a common male name, so the feminine pronoun *her* is incorrect. (Lesson 3)

8. The correct answers are:

kites/they

Paul and I/we

fishermen/they

company/it

deer/it

deer/they

Kites, Paul and I, and *fishermen* are all plural, so the plural pronouns *they, we*, and *they* are correct. Companies are not people, so they take the neutral pronoun *it. Deer* is trickier, but is right in both instances—because *deer* is an irregular noun, the plural and the singular are the same, meaning that both *it* and *they* can be correct. (Lesson 3)

9. The interrogative pronouns are *who, whom, whoever, whose, which*, and *whatever*. All of these pronouns can be used to begin questions. Who called me? Which is yours? To whom did he talk at the party? Whoever will be hired to fill the open position? *Where, when*, and *how* are adverbs. (Lesson 3)

10. The answers are:

⬚They⬚ *gave me the Miss Congeniality award!*

⬚She⬚ *never seems to have time to visit her old neighborhood.*

⬚We⬚ *picked a lot of peaches from our trees.*

Subjective pronouns are pronouns that act as the subject of a sentence, without another noun as an antecedent. *They, she*, and *we* are all the subjects of these sentences, even though there are no clearly associated nouns. (Lesson 3)

11. The correct answers are:

We lent ⬚it⬚ *to* ⬚him⬚.

Give ⬚me⬚ *a sign.*

He cooked ⬚them⬚ *ravioli.*

In this question, you're looking for the opposite of the pronouns in question 10. The subjects of the sentences are *we* (the people lending), *you* (which is implied to be the person giving a sign), and *he* (the person cooking ravioli). The objects are the people or items that will be affected by the actions. The item being lent (*it*) is for *him*, the sign is for *me*, and the ravioli is for *them*. (Lesson 3)

12. The correct answers are:

Andrew questioned ⬚himself⬚ *about his decision to buy the treadmill.*

His decision about buying the treadmill was rash.

Heather ⬚herself⬚ *wondered what prompted him to buy it.*

Reflexive pronouns refer back to a person or object performing an action. In these sentences, the reflexive pronouns are *himself* and *herself* (Andrew questions *himself*, Heather wonders *herself*). The possessive pronouns (*his* and *his*) show to whom the object belongs. The decision is Andrew's in both sentences, so *his* is the possessive case pronoun in both cases. (Lesson 3)

13. The correct answers are:

> [This] isn't a good way to spend the money that you saved!
>
> Is [that] the neighbor who drove you home from the airport?

Demonstrative pronouns are pronouns that help you determine what, exactly, is being discussed. (Lesson 3)

14. The correct answers are *look, talk, help, cook, draw, itch, moisten.* These are all specific actions that you can envision. *Just* is an adjective or adverb, not a verb. *Be* is a linking verb, not an action verb. *Should* and *may* are helping verbs, not action verbs. And a *geranium* is a flower, which means it's a noun. (Lesson 4)

15. The correct answers are *can, will, are, could, would, am,* and *did.* Linking and helping verbs give you more information about the main verb and its tense. She *can* cook well (present). Sam *will* wash the car after he gets out of work (future). We *are* ready when you are (present). Selena *could/would* have gone to the store if they were out of milk (past). I *am* very excited about the debate (present). Marina *did* know the meeting was at 2:00, but she was late anyway (past). Of the other options, *take* is an action verb. *Now, not, never,* and *how* are adverbs. (Lesson 4)

16. The regular verbs are *injure, lock, carry,* and *untie.* All of them follow standard patterns in the past tense: *injure* becomes *injured, lock* becomes *locked, carry* becomes *carried,* and *untie* becomes *untied.* The irregular verbs are *write, hide, mow, drive, know, grow, cost,* and *throw.* Their past participles are less straightforward: *write* becomes *written, hide* becomes *hidden, mow* becomes *mown, drive* becomes *driven, know* becomes *known, grow* becomes *grown, cost* stays *cost,* and *throw* becomes *thrown.* (Lesson 5)

17. The correct answers are *lays, lain,* and *laid.* The first and third sentences have instances of objects being placed somewhere, which means that the correct verb will be versions of to *lay.* The second sentence requires the past participle of to *lie* (to be situated). (Lesson 5)

18. The correct answers are *setting, sat,* and *set.* To *set* means to place objects, like Janice is doing, and we are doing with our glasses. To *sit* means to *be seated* or *be situated* in a particular place, as Jim was. (Lesson 5)

19. The correct answers are *may, except,* and *hung.* In the first sentence, the speaker is asking for permission, not trying to determine whether something is possible, so *may* is the correct choice. In the second sentence, you already know that he answered all the other questions. That suggests that the last question is different, and therefore you're looking for *except.* In the third sentence, that the speaker is spending time with friends suggests that the circumstances have nothing to do with the gallows (*hanged*), so you can go with the irregular past participle of to *hang: hung.* (Lesson 5)

20. The correct answers are:

> ***am swimming:*** *present progressive*
> ***had swum:*** *past perfect*
> ***will have swum:*** *future perfect*
> ***swam:*** *past*
> ***have swum:*** *present perfect*
> ***will swim:*** *future*
> ***were swimming:*** *past progressive*
> ***swims:*** *present*

Swim is an irregular verb, but you can still figure out the tense based on the words around the verb. The helping verb *am* tells you that *am swimming* is the present progressive tense. The helping verb *had* is your indicator for the past perfect tense, and *will have* indicates the future perfect tense. If you're familiar with the irregular verbs from Lesson 5, you'll recall that the past tense of *swim* is *swam*. The helping verb *have* plus the past participle *swum* tells you that you're working with the present perfect tense. *Will* plus the present tense *swim* lets you know that the swimming will happen in the future. The helping verb *were* plus the present participle *swimming* indicates that the action happened at a specific point in the past, which points to the past progressive. And *swims* is the present tense. (Lesson 6)

21. The common adjectives are *laptop, longtime, popular, legendary,* and *rock-and-roll. Laptop* describes *computer,* and *longtime* describes *friend. Popular* describes *sport. Legendary* and *rock-and-roll* both describe *performer.* None of these are specific names or otherwise proper titles, so they are common adjectives. (Lesson 7)

22. The correct answers are:

> ***a*** *hen*
> ***an*** *honorable person*
> ***a*** *one-car family*
> ***an*** *orthodontist*
> ***a*** *honeybee*
> ***an*** *orangutan*
> ***an*** *ozone layer*
> ***an*** *umbrella*
> ***an*** *hour-long lecture*
> ***a*** *universe*
> ***a*** *wristwatch*
> ***an*** *upperclassman*
> ***an*** *elegant dinner*
> ***an*** *underwater city*
> ***an*** *opinion*

As you may recall, the quickest way to determine indefinite articles is to sound out the nouns they modify. Words that start with a vowel (or a vowel sound) call for *an.* The letter *h* makes things tricky—but remember that if the *h* is silent, like in *honorable* or *hour,* go with *an;* if the *h* is not silent, like in *hen,* go with *a.* Words that start with a consonant (or sound like they start with a consonant, like the *w* sound of *one*) call for *a.* (Lesson 7)

23. The proper adjectives are *Samoan, Irish, Canadian, Washingtonian,* and *Antarctic.* Also, *Paris* and *Milwaukee* are proper nouns that may also act as proper adjectives (e.g., *Paris* museums). Proper adjectives are descriptive proper nouns that tell you about another noun. It should be clear that the proper names are describing other words, and aren't just stand-alone proper nouns. Common suffixes of proper adjectives are *-ian, -ish,* and *-an*—but you should remember that there are irregular proper adjectives that don't always follow this pattern. As with irregular verbs and nouns, you should try to memorize the exceptions. (Lesson 7)

24. The correct answers are:

>*my: possessive adjective*
>*his: possessive pronoun*
>*her: possessive adjective*
>*hers: possessive pronoun*
>*our: possessive adjective*
>*theirs: possessive pronoun*

To help tell the difference, look at what follows the pronoun. If a noun follows (like *coin collection*, *kindness*, and *hunch*), the pronoun is likely a possessive adjective. In the first sentence, *my* shows you to whom the coin collection belongs, which makes *my* possessive. It helps answer the question *which one?* Possessive pronouns, like *his*, *hers*, and *theirs*, are not followed by a noun. (Lesson 7)

25. The correct answers are:

>*that: demonstrative adjective*
>*those: demonstrative pronoun*
>*this: demonstrative pronoun*

As with question 24, apply the same test: what follows the demonstrative word? If it's another noun, then the demonstrative word is an adjective. If not, it's a demonstrative pronoun. (Lesson 7)

26. The correct answers are *coolest*, *slimier*, and *narrowest*. Remember that when it comes to comparatives and superlatives, use *-est* (superlative ending) when more than two things are being compared (like days of the week or all shoes). When only two things are being compared, like two rocks, the adjective is comparative rather than superlative, so *-er* is the proper suffix. (Lesson 7)

27. The correct answers are *most cautiously*, *longer*, and *better*. When more than two items are being compared (as with the three jockeys in the first sentence), choose the superlative (*most cautiously*). If two items are being compared (as with the two flights in the second sentence and my pie/Sam's mom's pie in the third sentence), choose the comparative adverb (*longer* and *better*, respectively). (Lesson 8)

28. The correct answers are adjective, adjective, and adverb. To figure out which is which, you need to look at the words being modified. In the first sentence, *hard* describes *Joe*, a noun—and this makes it an adjective. In the second sentence, *close* modifies *quarters*, a noun, which makes it an adjective. In the third sentence, *straight* modifies *went*, a verb—and thus it is an adverb. (Lessons 7 and 8)

29. The correct answers are *around the building*, *without a word*, *to his room*, and *around the back*. To find prepositional phrases, make sure you've familiarized yourself with the common prepositions (Lesson 9). Then, when you see one of them in a sentence followed by a noun or noun phrase, you know it's a prepositional phrase. In these sentences, the key words are *around* (followed by the nouns *building* and *back*), *without* (followed by the noun *word*), and *to* (followed by the noun *room*). (Lesson 9)

30. The correct answers are adverb (*around*), adverb (*out*), and preposition (*across*). If the common preposition in the sentence modifies a noun or pronoun (like *room* in the third sentence), then it introduces an official prepositional phrase. If the word stands alone and is not followed by a noun, it's an adverb. (Lesson 9)

31. The correct answers are:

>*The chef threw the roast, which was burned to a crisp, into the sink.*
>*Crocks of onion soup dripping with cheese were served to the guests.*
>*When Kerry was five, her parents brought her to Disney World.*

In the first sentence, you need to make clear that it was the roast, not the chef, that was burned to a crisp. In the second sentence, is the soup dripping with cheese, or are the guests? Were Kerry's parents five years old, or was Kerry? By making sure that modifiers are placed near the nouns they're modifying, you make the sentence and its meaning much clearer. (Lesson 10)

32. The correct answers are:

herd/heard	*just/just*
address/address	*coast/coast*
trip/trip	*real/reel*
died/dyed	*conduct/conduct*

(Lesson 10)

33. The simple subjects are *animals, artificial intelligence, [you], most,* and *Mike.* The subject is the person or object that is performing the action of the sentence. What is called nocturnal? *Animals.* What is used for games and medical purposes? *Artificial intelligence.* Who should stop? *You* (or rather, the person to whom the speaker is talking). Who liked it? *Most.* Who lives on his own and comes home once in a while? *Mike.* To help you identify the subject of a sentence, locate the nouns or pronouns, and determine whether they tell you what the sentence is about. (Lesson 11)

34. The simple predicates are *played, stand,* and *spotted.* The simple predicate is the verb that shows the action in the sentence, and these are all action verbs. (Lesson 11)

35. The correct answers are:

pieces: *direct object*
sheriff: *indirect object*
ovation: *direct object*
finalists: *indirect object*
time: *direct object*

(Lesson 11)

36. The correct answers are:

bad: *predicate adjective*
birds: *predicate noun*
chef: *predicate noun*

Predicate adjectives describe the subject, which *bad* does (describing the *sandwich*). Predicate nouns rename the subject. *Cockatiels* are also *birds,* and *Judy* was also a *chef.* (Lesson 11)

37. The correct answers are *is, try,* and *is. Bacon and eggs* may seem plural, but they really work together as one noun (a dish). In the second sentence, *Kara and Maria* (two separate people) are plural, so they take the plural present-tense verb *try.* In the third sentence, the *or* tells you that you are dealing with a single subject (either *science fiction* or *mystery,* not both). (Lesson 12)

38. The correct answers are *goes, needs,* and *prefers.* Look closely at the subjects of the sentences (which, in these cases, are indefinite pronouns). *Everyone, something,* and *each* are all singular, so they take the singular present-tense third-person verb (*goes, needs, prefers*). (Lesson 12)

39. The correct answers are *its, his or her,* and *its.* In the first sentence, the subject *the group* is singular, and therefore calls for the singular possessive *its.* In the second sentence, the subject *everyone* is singular—but from the context of the sentence, you can't tell whether the people involved are male or female, so you should go with *his or her.* In the third sentence, the subject is singular, but a *puppy* is an animal, so it takes the neutral possessive *its.* (Lesson 12)

40. The correct answers are:

of the shoes: *adjective phrase*
on the far shelf: *adverb phrase*
within the hour: *adverb phrase*
from the wall: *adverb phrase*

Remember to ask: What is the prepositional phrase modifying? In the first sentence, *of the shoes* describes *some* (a pronoun), so it is an adjective phrase. *On the far shelf* describes the location of the shoes; because it answers the question *where?,* it is an adverb phrase. Likewise, *within the hour* in the second sentence answers the question *when?,* making that an adverb phrase as well. In the third sentence, *from the wall* tells you *where* the picture was, so it too is an adverb phrase. (Lesson 13)

41. The correct answers are:

> ***becoming an accomplished pianist:*** *gerund phrase*
> ***to avoid slipping on the ice:*** *infinitive phrase*
> ***leaving his entire fortune to his nephew Lewis:*** *participial phrase*

Gerund phrases start with a gerund—an *-ing* verb acting as a noun—just as *becoming an accomplished pianist* does in the first sentence. In the second sentence, *to* tells you that you're working with an infinitive phrase. In the third sentence, the present-tense *leaving his entire fortune* acts as an adjective describing Zach, making it a participial phrase. (Lesson 13)

42. The correct answers are *the head of our science department*, *a professional tennis player*, and *the first state to ratify the U.S. Constitution*. Remember that an appositive phrase tells you more detail about a noun or pronoun in a sentence. In the first sentence, *the head of our science department* tells you more about Professor Williams. In the second sentence, *a professional tennis player* tells you more about Billie Jean King. In the third sentence, *the first state to ratify the U.S. Constitution* tells you more about Delaware. (Lesson 13)

43. The correct answers are:

> ***as I said:*** *subordinate clause*
> ***I am learning ballroom dancing:*** *independent clause*
> ***here are some for you:*** *independent clause*
> ***well, I should say so:*** *independent clause*
> ***that's life:*** *independent clause*
> ***stop that:*** *independent clause*

The best way to determine whether something is an independent clause is to see if it can stand as a sentence on its own. If the clause leaves you hanging (*as I said . . . what did you say?*), then it's a subordinate clause that relies on an independent clause to tell you what's going on in the sentence. Independent clauses have a clear subject and predicate. (Lesson 14)

44. The adjective clauses are *that my mom sang*, *who is at the end of the line*, and *where they sell many exotic fruits*. Adjective clauses act as adjectives to describe a noun or pronoun. In the first sentence, *that my mom sang* modifies *song*. In the second sentence, *who is at the end of the line* modifies *boy*. In the third sentence, *where they sell many exotic fruits* modifies *market*. (Lesson 14)

45. The noun clauses are *that drinking water is better than drinking soda*, *what time the store opens*, and *which shoes to wear*. Noun clauses are groups of words that, together, stand in for a single noun as part of a sentence. In the first sentence, *that drinking water is better than drinking soda* is the direct object of the verb *know*. In the second sentence, *what time the store opens* is also the object of the verb *know*. In the third sentence, *which shoes to wear* is the object of the verb *decide*. (Lesson 14)

46. The adverb clauses are *while we walked back*, *whether or not you believe it*, and *since her grandparents would be visiting*. Remember, adverb clauses are subordinate clauses that answer *where*, *when*, *how*, or *why*. In the first sentence, *while we walked back* tells you *when* we got wet. In the second sentence, *whether or not you believe it* answers the question of *how* the decision is yours. In the third sentence, *since her grandparents would be visiting* tells you more about *why* Violet decided to go home for the holidays. (Lesson 14)

47. The correct answers are:

> ***or*** (connects *gold* and *blue*)
> ***and*** (connects *Danielle* and *Joanna*)
> ***and*** (connects *watched a movie*, *popped popcorn*, and *stayed up all night talking*)
> ***so*** (connects *Sometimes we go to the lake* and *we can water-ski*)

Remember the acronym FANBOYS (*for*, *and*, *nor*, *but*, *or*, *yet*, *so*). Once you have those down, you can find them quickly within sentences and see which elements they connect. (Lesson 15)

48. The correct answers are:
    a. compound
    b. compound-complex
    c. simple
    d. complex

Sentence **a** contains two subjects (*some citizens* and *many*) and two predicates (*voted in the town election* and *did not*), so it is a compound sentence. Sentence **b** contains two independent clauses (*just add butter and milk to the boiled potatoes* and *mash until creamy*) and a subordinate clause (*if you want to make mashed potatoes*), which makes it a compound-complex sentence. Sentence **c** has a single subject (the implied *you*) and a single predicate (*put your folded laundry away, please*); it is one independent clause, so it is a simple sentence. Sentence **d** has one subordinate clause (*because Jill was late*) and one independent clause (*she missed the introductory overview of the entire workshop*), so it is a complex sentence. (Lesson 16)

49. The correct answers are:
    On April 12, 1861, the Civil War began with the battle at Fort Sumter.
    The dentist's hygienists and staff threw a surprise party for him.
    Would you consider using Benji's or Jess's racket for now?

In the first sentence, use a comma to separate the day and the year, and add a comma after *1861* to set the year off with commas and to conclude the introductory phrase. As always, you should make sure that your sentence ends with proper punctuation; this sentence isn't a question or an exclamation, so it ends with a period. In the second sentence, make sure it's clear that the hygienists and staff belong to the dentist, and place the possessive apostrophe accordingly (after determining whether the sentence is about a single dentist or a group of dentists). And again, make sure that the end punctuation is in place—in this case (a common statement), it's a period. In the third sentence, the racket belongs to the Benji or Jess, so you need possessive apostrophes. Double-*s* words can be tricky, but three *s*'s in a row tell you that something is wrong—and given that *Jess* is a singular noun, you know that it should get the singular, possessive -*'s*. This sentence is also missing end punctuation. The helping verb *would* at the beginning of the sentence tells you that a question is being asked, so the correct end punctuation is a question mark. (Lessons 17–20)

50. The correct answers are:

> *"It's not easy to memorize all of the mathematical formulas for algebra," stated Mrs. Shapiro, "but we'll accomplish that by the year's end."*
>
> *"Would you make my steak sandwich without onions, please?" asked Harry.*
>
> *"I," began Courtney, "am not the only girl who feels that way."*

In these sentences, it's important to read through and separate the parts of the sentences to make it clear who is talking and what they are saying. In the first sentence, *stated Mrs. Shapiro* tells you that it's a direct quote, but the *we'll* that follows suggests that the quote starts up again after pausing in the middle to tell you who is speaking. So it's important to set off the middle section (*stated Mrs. Shapiro*) with commas and to be sure that each section of the full quote begins and ends with quotation marks. The second sentence ends with *asked Harry*, telling you that everything that comes before that point is part of Harry's question. In addition to placing the quotation marks correctly so that you know what Harry is asking, it's also key to add the correct end punctuation to the quote: a question mark. The third sentence, like the first, pauses within the quote to let you know who is speaking, so it's important to figure out what Courtney is saying directly and how she is saying it. (Lessons 17–20)

ADDITIONAL ONLINE PRACTICE ▶

Whether you need help building basic skills or preparing for an exam, visit the LearningExpress Practice Center! On this site, you can access additional practice materials. Using the code below, you'll be able to log in and get additional grammar practice. This online practice will also provide you with:

- **Immediate scoring**
- **Detailed answer explanations**
- **Personalized recommendations for further practice and study**

Log in to the LearningExpress Practice Center by using this URL: **www.learnatest.com/practice**

This is your Access Code: **9315**

Follow the steps online to redeem your access code. After you've used your access code to register with the site, you will be prompted to create a username and password. For easy reference, record them here:

Username: _____ **Password:** _____

With your username and password, you can log in and answer these practice questions as many times as you like. If you have any questions or problems, please contact LearningExpress customer service at 1-800-295-9556 ext. 2, or e-mail us at **customerservice@learningexpressllc.com**.

NOTES

NOTES

NOTES

NOTES